ENVIRONMENTAL COMPLIANCE

THE CHANDOS SERIES ON THE ENVIRONMENT

ENVIRONMENTAL COMPLIANCE

The Business Benefits

Ben Vivian

SGS United Kingdom Ltd.

CP

Chandos Publishing (Oxford) Limited

ISBN 1 902375 11 4

Chandos Publishing (Oxford) Limited
Chandos House
5 & 6 Steadys Lane
Stanton Harcourt
Oxford OX8 1RL
England

Tel: 01865 884447 Fax: 01865 884448

Printed in England

DEDICATION

For Sarah

Contents

FOREWORD

I have known and worked with Ben Vivian for many years now and I am delighted that he has made it into print with this practical guide on the 'how' of improved environmental performance.

While he worked with us here at Nabarro's it was quite apparent that our clients not only valued his depth of knowledge and sheer enthusiasm for his subject, but also benefited from his direct, unfussy, hands-on approach to their problems. Importantly, given that he was working for a law firm, Ben had (and still has) a healthy respect for the legal 'drivers' behind improved environmental performance. However, he rightly sees beyond purely legal influences and in this book takes into account other drivers of change such as global, social or market forces.

It is these additional factors which have given much of the impetus for the development of the EMAS and ISO environmental management systems and which also persuade many responsible organisations to 'go that extra mile' and so reap the full benefits. I am sure that all who read this book will learn and benefit from Ben's acknowledged expertise and experience in corporate environmental management, and I commend it to you.

Mike Renger
Head of Environment Department
Nabarro Nathanson
1 South Quay
Victoria Quays
Sheffield S2 5SY

PREFACE

This book contains some of the many areas of business compliance – but cannot contain them all. The selection process has been somewhat subjective; areas covered are those I consider to be of most relevance to the widest business audience. It might be a surprise to some readers that there is little detail given to Integrated Pollution Control, perhaps the most important piece of environmental legislation, but one affecting only a limited number of UK companies. I have, though, given some space to what will take over from those regulations in 1999.

For environmental compliance to be truly delivered it is necessary to deal with future and newly enacted regulations. The future will see a gradual but radical shift in environmental compliance. This future must be addressed with a clear sight on a compliant goal.

I do not believe that environmental issues will disappear because international, national and local political concern will continue to drive new legal instruments and regulatory structures. But, perhaps, more important is the range of initiatives being considered by other parties, either with or without commercial focus. Some of these new initiatives are covered in Chapter 3.

Environmental compliance provides a management focus that can bring short and longer-term benefits. Most important is the much greater commercial security that results from such a focus. The processes described provide a more inclusive approach to doing successful business in the local and wider community. One very positive feature of environmental initiatives is the change from businesses as inward looking, reactive organisations to ones that view the wider world as an integral part of their future.

I hope to provide, through these pages, a useful resource, not a checklist or manual (in its strict sense), but a simple vehicle to allow business managers to think. In a busy world we all spend too little time thinking and too much time chasing our tails. A small investment of time can provide an opportunity to address challenges in a positive manner. I certainly found that making time — needed to set out the ideas in this book very worthwhile — to prepare, order and reorder, research and talk to a range of fascinating people and, of course, spend time thinking and reading. I found the process very valuable personally and professionally.

I would welcome feedback on the book because I am not suggesting that it should be considered the only approach. It can be refined and improved, but at the moment this book represents what I believe to be a useful, inclusive way of thinking about and managing the real issues in this complex process.

Dr Ben Vivian
April 1999

ACKNOWLEDGEMENTS

There are numerous people who have had to listen to my half baked ideas before they could be put down on paper. The environment world is still a relatively small place, so I beg forgiveness if I have missed anyone.

First, I would like to thank Mike Renger, Michael Morris and Anna Marshall who provided me with excellent grounding and refinement in environmental law while I was Technical Environmental Advisor at Nabarro Nathanson. I invited Mike Renger to write the foreword in recognition of this experience.

Secondly, Patrick Mallon (Business in the Environment) with whom I have collaborated successfully over the past five years on many projects and with whom many solutions to the world's troubles have been discussed over a beer.

Thirdly, I would like to thank those who have had a direct input into the research and preparation of the material in the book: Andy Gouldson (LSE); Craig Mackenzie (Friends Provident); Martin Blaxall (BG plc); Dr Andrea Coulson (Durham University Business School); Iain Gardiner (English Welsh Scottish Railway); and Mallen Baker (Business in the Environment).

Finally, I would like to thank my new colleagues at SGS United Kingdom Ltd, most particularly David Warlow, Jeff Dowson, David Clark and Dr Grant Richardson.

THE AUTHOR

Dr Ben Vivian is a Senior Consultant with SGS United Kingdom Ltd, Environment Division. He has a wide range of experience in the environment discipline. He graduated from the University of Hull with a degree in Geography in 1984. After a year teaching geography at King's School Worcester he returned to university to study for a DPhil with Dr Tim Burt at Keble College, Oxford. The research continued a long held interest in slope stability and soil hydrology. On leaving Oxford, he became a researcher, studying nitrate movement in agricultural soils at the Scottish Agricultural College in Edinburgh, then solute transport at Silsoe College. While at Silsoe he joined the newly formed Cranfield Environment, which was establishing multidisciplinary teams to develop environmental audit methodology. This was extended at Hull University, where he developed and delivered courses for local businesses in environmental awareness and law.

In 1995 a post at Nabarro Nathanson was established for him by Mike Renger, where he worked for a variety of clients, including the Coal Authority, Jarvis Facilities Ltd, Loadhaul Ltd, the Earth Centre, Croda International plc, Harrisons and Crosfield plc, waste management companies and Millennium Chemicals Ltd. Most of his experience is in the UK but he has worked in Spain, Bulgaria and the Czech Republic.

Since joining SGS in April 1998 he has continued to work with clients trying to improve performance and to get the most out of systems and their people. He has already developed and worked on many projects with clients including: EWS Railway, Biffa Waste Services Ltd, Sanyo Ltd, Thames Water plc, Castrol International, Bechtel Ltd and Nottingham City Council. He is also visiting lecturer at the University of Nottingham, lecturing on the Environmental Management MSc programme. His philosophy is based heavily on working with people rather than imposing technological solutions to address environmental problems. He specialises in five distinct areas: environmental compliance auditing, EMS development and auditing, environmental reporting, training development and delivery, and strategic advice.

Ben has been married for ten years to Dr Sarah Metcalfe, reader in Physical Geography at Edinburgh University, who specialises in acid rain and climate change research and teaching. The topic of the environment is never far from view

The author may be contacted at the following address:

SGS United Kingdom Ltd.

Environment Division

2 Hutton Close Business Centre

South Church Enterprise Park

Bishop Auckland

County Durham DL14 6XG

Telephone: 01388-776677

Fax: 01388-776691

CHAPTER 1

Introduction to Environmental Compliance

Changing Scope of Environmental Issues Facing Business

Twenty years ago the scientific community was warning against a forthcoming environmental disaster – the next ice age. How times and the message have changed. In the natural environment change occurs all the time – we could call it evolution. The pace of this change is slow and adaptation has occurred without interference from human activities. We are a relatively recent factor that natural ecosystems have had to contend with – relative in terms of geological time-scales.

In the latter part of the twentieth century we are beginning to see the effects of our technological and societal interference in our planet's complex and evolving ecosystems. Over the past twenty years we have had to become aware of a vast range of issues that have all been lumped together under the general heading of 'environment issues'. We have been told about the 'hole in the ozone layer', 'the greenhouse effect', 'climate change and global warming' (the latter term thankfully is beginning to disappear from our vocabulary), 'water resource pollution and depletion', 'desertification', 'non-renewable resource conservation', 'air pollution', 'acid rain', 'tropical rainforest destruction'...the list is seemingly endless. The effects of our activities are still only partially understood in all of these issues. Yet the call for action has increased in volume and it is often directed at the business community. But what should we be doing to counteract our negative effects and promote our positive effects on the environment? All of our activities have either a positive or negative effect on the environment around us.

We should not restrict ourselves by thinking that we have only recently begun to have an impact on our environment as a species. There is growing evidence that pre-industrial societies had significant environmental impacts in their own small patches of the planet. The image of the environmentally 'benign savage' is now being questioned. What has changed is that our activities have become increasingly extensive and complex. Perhaps most important is the pace of our change, which does not allow natural systems to respond or evolve.

The message is that change in our planet's ecosystems is inevitable. But this does not allow us to close our eyes and ears to the changes. Some of the issues listed above appear to be out of our immediate control or influence, but everyone has a positive role to play in environmental issues. The issue for the business community is no longer why, but how can we take action to make our individual contributions.

What Is Environmental Compliance?

Environmental compliance is concerned with understanding the nature of an organisation, its processes, people, impact, products and services, and community interactions, then developing and implementing standards of performance in order to meet the requirements of a range of expectations from various stakeholders. The problem (or challenge) is to simplify the complexity of the task and overcome the general lack of standardised and accepted information, criteria or methods against which to test the level of compliance of an organisation.

The process of environmental compliance may begin with an understanding of the requirements of the law (Chapter 2) as it directly affects the operations of an organisation, but it goes beyond that if comprehensive compliance is to be achieved (Chapter 3). Environmental risk is clearly an issue which will be considered throughout this book, but again this is only one of the many tools and methods which an organisation may use in the goal of compliant status. Environmental management systems are becoming an increasingly popular business tool for environmental performance improvement and thus achieve a higher level of compliance. There are legal and societal compliance issues integral with this new area, which are addressed in Chapter 4.

Environmental performance improvements are increasingly an external issue requiring more and more internal resources. Pressure from policy-makers, regulators, shareholders, neighbours, customers and employees are the most obvious (and most frequently cited). Banks, lenders and other financial institutions are growing in awareness and confidence when addressing environmental issues.

Developing Benefits from Environmental Compliance

It is difficult to provide a simple view of this complex business issue. But in order for the benefits to be delivered we need to identify a model which can help to describe the necessary elements of the process for improvement. Figure 1.1 describes the relationship between three factors – compliance, benefits and time-scale. Most businesses are in block A where legal compliance is viewed as a short-term issue and business benefits are realised predominantly from cost-savings derived from waste minimisation initiatives. Of the seven remaining options B remains elusive to most companies because of a lack of awareness of the long-term and non-statutory compliance issues (explored in Chapter 3) and the perceived risk of taking the first step towards this uncertain future. In order to achieve the added benefits in B the underlying message is increased awareness and access to information of the non-statutory, emerging issues from a wide range of sources.

Figure 1.1 Compliance, Business Benefits and Time-scale

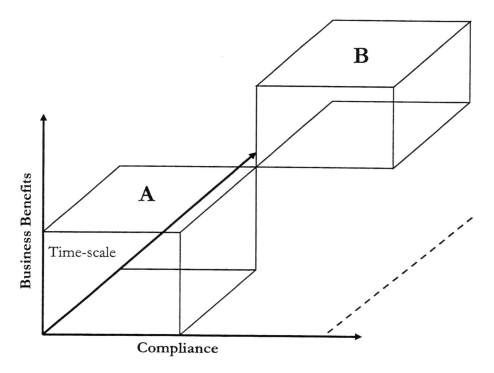

Most businesses are in Block A. If close to the origin, they view environmental compliance as a short-term issue which provides few business benefits. As awareness grows and waste minimisation initiatives are implemented they move up the y-axis (vertical), but remain rooted in current legislation as the only targets worthy of attention. A business which starts to adopt strategies to plan for the effects of new legislation then moves out along the z-axis. All of these elements of environmental compliance are addressed to a greater or lesser degree in Chapter 2.

Box B remains the most elusive of the remaining possible options. A lack of awareness of the business benefits provided by complying with non-statutory issues prevents movement towards this ultimate positioning.

The book seeks to raise initial awareness of the issues. In doing so and providing examples of what benefits exist, I hope to demonstrate some of the possibilities presented for those who move away from the origin. It could be argued that many of these benefits are intangible using traditional economic measures. But with growing concern and as the development of methods of assuaging those concerns becoming mainstream, so the maximum business and environmental benefits can be realised.

Fundamental Tenets of Environmental Compliance

A key goal of this book is to review the processes of compliance in a commercial context. The fundamental benefit for a business of achieving environmental compliance is commercial security. There are other secondary benefits, many of which will be explored in this book.

The degree of compliance obtained by an organisation is a function of the level of control it exerts, which in turn is based on the level of understanding of the myriad of environmental issues and their impacts.

So environmental compliance is a two-phase process:

•   gaining appropriate knowledge – or what;

•   putting into practice the improvements and sustaining them – or how.

This book will not address, any further than that stated above, the reasons why. If we do not already know the answer to that question then we as a society are, I believe, in real trouble.

Gaining Benefits by Managing Change

In order to achieve business benefits from environmental compliance, we need to change how an organisation manages its activities. Further, to stimulate this change we need to be clear about the pressures, both positive and negative, which are exerted on that organisation. These pressures push or pull an organisation to change and are dealt with effectively in other books or articles – a selection has been included as further reading.

Over the past ten years society has raised its expectations of what is required from the business community in respect of how it interacts with the environment. This requirement has placed much emphasis on increasing the levels of awareness of our impact on the environment. The concern for our environment has led to a number of responses from a wide range of different individuals, organisations and institutions.

- The formulation of new laws and processes of regulation which have an impact in terms of operational management and planning in many organisations.

- Financial and environmental risk has led lenders and insurers to seek more detailed information from those borrowing money or seeking insurance cover.

- Innovation in the money and investment markets has produced new products which seek to favour organisations with proven good performance and commitment to improvement.

- Technological advances have driven up standards of expected and desired performance both as a legal requirement (e.g. BATNEEC, defined in Chapter 2) and as an issue of competitiveness.

- Sources of non-renewable resources are threatened by unsustainable exploitation, and so alternative resources or production practices become a commercial necessity.

- Public (and other stakeholder) pressure to be more open and accountable about past, present and future performance in terms of environmental impacts.

- Employees are increasingly concerned and will not necessarily accept wanton and persistent poor performance.

Each of these concerns or changes of circumstance requires an alteration in performance and management of an organisation. Accountability, not only on environmental matters, is a growing public and political topic for debate. Where the environment is a matter of concern, it is important to note that all of us have a view as to what is or is not acceptable behaviour. What we lack, with some exceptions, is an accurate set of accepted standards against which to judge performance or assess compliance.

What this book sets out to do is to address the multitude of environmental compliance issues from a practical, solution-based approach. No longer is it a wise commercial decision to bury one's head in the sand and hope that all the fuss will disappear. The range of environmental compliance issues will deepen and broaden – and will almost certainly change the nature of activities required for compliance. I hope to be able to show that complexity can be simplified and that commercial benefits exist for those that look for them.

As the techniques, necessary to deliver compliance with the various environmental standards and requirements (legal or otherwise), are developed and become more sophisticated, so the process of delivery becomes an integrated part of business or organisational management. It is quite clear that, while specialist knowledge is required, the process of understanding what is required for compliance is part of mainstream business thinking and management strategy. If we as an industrial society are to achieve the improvements necessary to allow survival (which I hope is not putting it too dramatically) and development, then all of us need to be involved. Environmental compliance must be inclusive and cannot be confused by exclusive professional jargon. We need to develop and use business management systems and practices which are entirely inclusive – if we are to produce sustained improvement.

The cry that is heard frequently from businesses is not why change – we now all know why – but how do we change. This change must happen at no net loss to overall performance of the organisation and preferably it should provide benefits. In order to understand how, we must first look in more detail at drivers for and barriers to change.

Many surveys in the past 5 years have identified the drivers, such as the Groundwork Report on *Small Firms and the Environment*. Figure 1.2 reproduces the results of the Gallup survey performed as part of the research. Cost savings and regulatory pressure are the usual leading drivers – in this and many other studies. These are addressed elsewhere in this book.

Figure 1.2 Factors Effective in Motivating Small and Medium-sized Enterprises (SMEs) to Adopt Environmental Policy (*Source:* Gallup SME Attitude Survey in Small Firms and the Environment by Groundwork Trust)

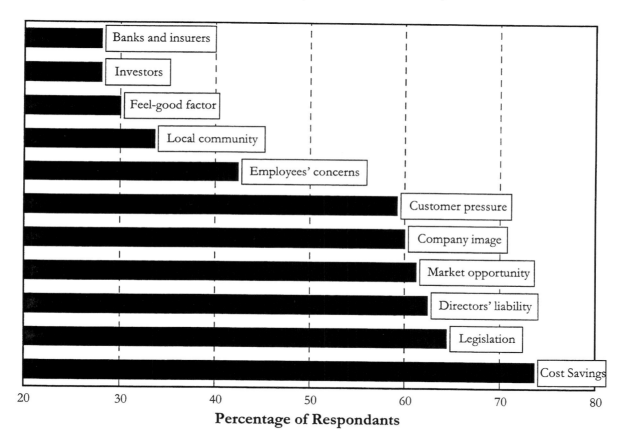

It is more important to understand the nature and significance of the various barriers when addressing change management. If we simply assume that the drivers are effective in producing change, then sadly we are deluding ourselves. It is apparent that the majority of organisations are simply not interested or those which have started improvement programmes and reaped the commercial gains are only tinkering at the edges.

The barriers to change are important to understand for any professional or environmental manager attempting to undertake a process of environmental compliance. A discussion of the barriers which exist in each case will improve our understanding of the challenge. Table 1.1 sets out these barriers to change.

Table 1.1 Barriers Restricting Opportunities for Change

Issue	Barrier
Cost Saving	• Most businesses are not profit motivated (especially Small and Medium-sized Enterprises or SMEs) – they are sales or turnover motivated. • External experts are directly criticising current practices. • 'If we have success as we are now, why change?' • 'I don't have the time or resources to do it now'.
Legislation and Regulatory Pressure	• Ignorance. • Most organisations rarely have direct contact with regulatory agencies. • Low risk of prosecution has created an attitude of 'it won't happen to me'.
Directors' Liability	• As above.
Market Opportunity	• Radical innovation is not a high priority for many companies – especially SMEs – and demonstrates the reducing level of investment in R & D by UK firms. • Generally business is risk averse.
Positive Company Image	• This is a big company issue usually based around crisis management and risk prevention. Public attitude to environmental PR is generally poor. • SMEs are not concerned compared to the fight to survive.
Customer Pressure	• The surge of environmental questionnaires issued by large companies have not been followed up – resulting in accusations of superficiality.
Employees' Concerns	• Awareness still relatively low. • Fear of the consequences of 'whistle-blowing'.
Local Community Concerns	• People in the community don't complain if they work in local businesses. • Skill levels requiring employers to look beyond the neighbourhood.
Feel-good Factor	• Most businesses are more intent on survival and do not have, or do not feel that they have the time to consider such an issue.
Investors	• Most investors have not yet addressed environmental issues in a systematic and objective manner – though this is beginning to change.
Banks and Insurers	• A similar attitude to environmental issues as with investors.

If we take one of these drivers, the one that is most frequently top of the list, and look in some more detail at the barriers then we will begin to see the challenge facing businesses in achieving environmental compliance. A simple balance sheet (Table 1.2) can be used to convince business managers that improvement is going to benefit their financial bottom line.

Table 1.2 Cost Saving and the Effect on the Bottom Line

Turnover	£1,000,000
Profit	£100,000
Energy spend	£40,000
Anticipated savings – 20%	£8,000
Percentage improvement in profit (simple)	8%
Additional turnover required to deliver same percentage improvement	£80,000

It would appear to be common sense to assume that any managing director would look at this evidence and be impressed and motivated to adopt the necessary changes. It is, however, a fundamental economic dichotomy. Most economic theories describe the perfect, objective human being as a fundamental tenet. This clearly is not true. We are not only motivated by profit. Most businesses would rather put their effort into growing turnover – think about how a business describes performance. The primary indicator of performance is turnover, profit is a secondary indicator. In some types of small business, the family business for example, even turnover is only a secondary issue compared to other qualitative indicators such as employment.

This simple observation leads to the conclusion that cost saving as a key issue for business is not necessarily driven by a profit motive. Although Table 1.1 identifies other barriers to adopting cost savings, it is the internal competition between turnover and profit which will be subconsciously preventing a company gaining any benefit. It is perhaps beyond the scope of this book to discuss the implications of this revelation in terms of government policy towards environmental improvement – but it is a fundamental aspect that appears to have been ignored, or at least seen as unimportant.

In this book I shall look at a wide range of compliance issues and not make a simple assumption that costs saving is the only aspect of environmental performance improvement that delivers any commercial benefit.

Making Compliance a Positive

The message that I hope is emerging is that the process of addressing environmental issues in a business can be complex. But, as with the global environmental issues, complexity should not be an excuse for inactivity. A rational and objective approach based on sound understanding is what is required. If progress is to be made then the perception that industry and environment are incompatible needs to be dispelled. The former, a diverse set of institutions, and the latter, a set of issues that pose a threat to continued quality of life, need to be reconciled. There is growing recognition of this fact in the concept of ecological modernization.

> *Rather than perceiving environmental protection to be a brake on growth, ecological modernization promotes the application of stringent environmental policy as a positive influence on economic efficiency and technological innovation. Similarly, rather than perceiving economic development to be the cause of environmental decline, ecological modernization seeks to harness the forces of entrepreneurship for environmental gain.*
>
> (From page 1 of *Regulatory Realities* by Andrew Gouldson and Joseph Murphy, published by Earthscan, 1998.)

CHAPTER 2

Statutory Compliance

Introduction

Traditionally 'compliance' has meant compliance with environmental legislation, but as Chapter 3 will present the scope is rapidly expanding to include many environmental issues requiring compliance. It is, however, important to address legal issues before the myriad of other issues. The development of legislation designed to protect the environment has run in parallel with concerns in society and has given to us a set of standards, to a degree, which we can aim for and set objectives against. This legislation is an inevitable consequence of our inability to address the issues voluntarily. The imposition of control measures and regulatory structures has resulted in resentment in industrial sectors. This resentment can be blamed for the failure of many to address environmental compliance in a positive manner. It is not possible in this book to address all the legislation on the statute book, so I have taken a sample of common and important legislation. I have limited myself to environmental protection legislation and will not refer to planning law, which certainly has an impact on industrial activity, nor to habitat protection or conservation legislation.

This chapter will provide a description of the policy and legal framework which operates in the United Kingdom and includes case studies of positive and negative attitudes to statutory compliance. Each case contains analysis of the compliance issues and the internal management activities which led to success or failure. The cases presented are real, but due to the nature of the material the identity of the companies has been withheld. A simple outline of the legislation is included where it is considered important to the particular issue. Further reading is provided with texts covering the detail of the legislation.

Presenting a general discussion of environmental compliance requires some more detailed description of specific ways in which businesses can produce commercial benefits. In recent years attempts have been made to form environmental protection legislation which has broadened in scope to encompass a growing list of industrial and commercial activities. The move toward 'producer responsibility', for example, has resulted in legislation being drafted covering controlled waste regulation, packaging waste recovery and recycling. Both offer immediate and longer-term benefit to those organisations which understand the practical implications of these regulations on their operation. For a business to turn regulation to advantage, it must first clearly understand the application and then devise strategies which provide overall benefit – rather than always viewing regulation as an imposition from the state with inevitable cost implications. It remains a fact that some improvements will require capital expenditure. But costs can be offset if a business takes on a range of long-term improvements which over time and in combination produce direct financial and commercial benefits. Approaching environmental compliance in a 'piecemeal' manner may not offer any instant returns on what can be quite significant investment.

Direct benefit over the longer term may be gained, without moving into the indirect benefits presented by non-statutory compliance benefits (*see* Chapter 3), if due consideration and advice is sought. The immediate reactions to new or revised environmental regulations can be described as:

- more internal resources without benefit;

- greater capital expenditure without payback.

Neither of these immediate reactions needs to become reality if placed within an extensive programme of improved environmental and overall business efficiency.

Finally, this chapter will provide some information on the nature of emerging statutory controls. This content, by its nature, becomes dated. But I hope to show how a positive approach to new legislation can provide a company with an advantage over their competitors, and move it from box A into box B (Figure 1.1).

The Policy and Legal Framework

Any business seeking to gain the benefits from complying with environmental legislation should review the policy that sits behind the statutes that provide the detail. Although it appears remote from the everyday business activities, policy provides a number of simple indicators as to the direction of future legislation and background to existing laws. Figure 1.1 shows that increased business benefit can be gained by looking longer term and addressing compliance issues presented by future legislation.

The European Union increasingly sets environmental policy. There are some basic principles of the general policy:

- polluter pays;

- pollution prevention;

- consultation; and

- integration.

Although this is a gross simplification of what is a complex structure of policy mechanism, we can use these to improve our understanding of how to achieve compliance.

Polluter Pays

If we consider that pollution is an inevitable consequence of human activity, then someone should pay towards the costs of repairing the resulting damage of that pollution. A person causing pollution may be required to pay in a number of different ways:

- fines and other penalties;

- permits to operate (authorisations);

- permits to pollute (consents);

- clean-up and remediation;

- regulatory costs.

This principle can be expected to remain and the costs imposed on polluters to increase, in one or all of the above categories. Breaching environmental legislation is a criminal offence and carries with it the risk of fines and imprisonment when the matter goes to court. The cost of pollution can therefore be the loss of individual freedom – a rarity but it has happened in the UK on more than one occasion.

Pollution Prevention

In the past, emphasis was placed on controlling pollution. Now policy has moved away from 'end-of-pipe' control measures and concentrates on preventing pollution at its source. This principle can be seen in the waste hierarchy (Figure 2.1), which seeks to move our attention to less environmentally harmful methods of handling and managing our waste. Legislation is already in force which is designed to discourage control and encourage prevention. New legislation is now being drafted which will promote pollution prevention in industries previously only required to control their pollution – the Integrated Pollution Prevention and Control Directive (96/61/EC) is due to come into force in UK law in October 1999, and is described in greater detail later in this chapter.

Figure 2.1 A Version of the Waste Hierarchy

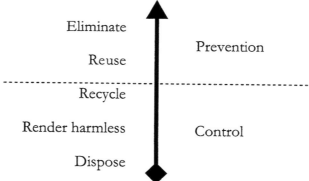

Consultation

At the heart of the government's approach to environmental protection is the need for consultation between the legislature and interested parties. This practice exists as recognition of the vast range of interested parties which may be affected by the legislation once it is in force. It is commonplace for draft legislation to go through a series of consultation phases before becoming a Bill to go before the Houses of Parliament. This consultation often includes companies and trade associations, as well as pressure groups and the general public. Consultation has long been a part of the planning process in the UK, and it is logical for environmental issues to require a similar process.

In practice consultation has two significant implications:

- information is disseminated which can be used as preparation for the impending changes; and

- laws reflect the stresses which can be exerted by parties with very different agendas.

The former presents obvious benefits to any business which is directly involved throughout the consultation process while the latter can result in extremely complex laws trying to take account of all the various parties' concerns.

Integration

There are now two simple forms of integration – internal integration and external integration.

- Internal integration means that policies are integrated to cover pollution of water, air and land – not a new concept in the UK since the introduction of Integrated Pollution Control in the Environmental Protection Act 1990.

- External integration is broader as it means integrating environmental considerations into other policy areas, such as transport, agriculture and energy. External integration has been practised for some time in the Netherlands and more recently a form of integration has occurred in the UK with the formation of the Department of Environment, Transport and the Regions (DETR).

Integration has also occurred in environmental protection regulation institutions. In 1976 the Royal Commission on Environmental Pollution published a report called 'Air Pollution Control: An Integrated Approach' which noted that because of the connections between different forms of industrial pollution it made little sense to look at one aspect in isolation. The UK government at first rejected the idea, but then in 1987 changed its mind when it formed the 'unified' pollution inspectorate, Her Majesty's Inspectorate of Pollution (or HMIP). With the Environmental Protection Act 1990, HMIP was given powers under IPC to grant a single authorisation for certain 'prescribed processes', covering discharges to air and water and the generation of waste. This enabled HMIP to encourage industrialists to think about their process as a whole and to promote 'cleaner technology'. By applying best available techniques not entailing excessive cost (BATNEEC) the releases of prescribed substances could be controlled and used to minimise pollution of the environment as a whole (see below).

The creation of the Environment Agency in 1996 was a further step to integration. HMIP, the National Rivers Authority and the waste regulatory functions of local authorities were combined (but without major changes to their powers).

European Legislation

There are a number of forms of legislative tools used by the European Union. These include regulations, directives and decisions. The first two are the most common and relevant to businesses, because decisions relate to very specific issues of law.

- Regulations: immediately binding on Member States and are automatically incorporated into national law;

- Directives: binding as to the purpose to be achieved, but have to be implemented by the Member States either through the creation of new Acts and Regulations or by amending existing ones.

Directives are the most usual method for introducing new national legislation. A business which continuously reviews the progress of draft directives and implementation into UK law will be able to predict and take into account changes before they become law. Three years is now the standard period between a directive coming into force and Member States enacting new legislation (if the Member State's government is to comply with the relevant directive). A business which takes appropriate steps to keep up to speed on European legislation can have three to five years' head start over competitors – allowing capital expenditure to be phased and staff to be trained, among other things.

One basic problem remains, however. Directives contain very general information on details of performance and do not contain any prescriptions for the mechanisms to be adopted. If we look at the transposition of the Packaging and Packaging Waste Directive (94/62/EC) into the Producer Responsibility Obligations (Packaging Waste) Regulations 1997, then it is clear that the process of consultation (see comments above) and the peculiarities of Whitehall have resulted in a very complex structure of legislation, regulation and compliance options. The directive contains definitions of the key terms, instructions to Member States on the method of regulating the process, targets for the recovery and recycling of packaging waste, and cross reference to other relevant directives and treaties. The directive covers some 3-4 pages of text. The regulations in the UK are contained in some 80 pages, with two major additional guidance documents. Although the directive contains little detail as to the process the UK will adopt, it does have enough information to allow a business to formulate a strategy which would allow compliance, once it came into force in UK law, to be straightforward. Reading a directive, with assistance from legal or technical specialists as required, allows a business manager to draw out the i and t, without the dot and cross being provided until the national legislation is enacted and enforced.

Waste Duty of Care

The principle of duty of care is not a new legal concept. It can apply to many aspects of health and safety and property management. In terms of waste management, section 34 of the Environmental Protection Act 1990 (EPA90) can provide a range of business and operational benefits. Some of these benefits, in terms of quantified cost savings, have been set out in various publications covering waste minimisation demonstration projects. The Aire and Calder Project (the first government supported waste minimisation scheme) and reports on the 3Es scheme developed by HMIP and Business in the Environment are examples of attempts to disseminate good practice and associated cost saving benefits.

Duty of care requires a producer of controlled waste to describe, store, treat, transfer and dispose of waste so that no harm (defined in section 1 of EPA90) is caused to the environment or human health. At its simplest, duty of care requires producers to identify clearly storage facilities, complete and sign off transfer notes and deal with registered waste management contractors. Further sophistication results in specific waste materials segregation and surveillance (or audit) of the operations of the contracted waste management company. Guidance is provided by environmental agencies to business in a Code of Practice. The Code does not, however, describe the processes necessary to generate environmental compliance with business benefits. Outlined below are real examples of good and bad performance in this area of compliance with an assessment made of the benefits gained or lost in each case. The cases are real but in most it is not possible accurately to quantify the benefit. The intention is to raise issues which the reader is familiar with but has not necessarily thought through the consequences.

Case One – Waste Not Accepted by Landfill

Company A had a skip containing some 200–300 fluorescent tubes produced during infrastructure maintenance programmes. The skip belonged to a small local hire company. When the waste contractor driver arrived at the location he presented an amended invoice – not a legal transfer note – and assured the responsible person that the skip's content could be disposed of and took the material off-site. The vehicle was followed and observed entering a local landfill – within two minutes the lorry returned with its load intact. Two options remained. The driver could fly-tip the load or return the skip and its contents to the site. On returning to the site with the load intact, the driver tore up the invoice, muttering that he had not had that sort of problem before.

The practical implications of this incident are that:

a)   the contractor was clearly unfit to handle the waste;

b)   the waste, nature and quantity, should have been pre-notified and handled as special waste – in compliance with appropriate regulations;

c)   site staff and supervisory managers were themselves unaware of the consequences of their actions and decisions;

d)   additional staff and management time was 'wasted' in disposing of the waste again – this time legally.

This case arose because of a combination of a), b) and c) above and the legal obligation correctly discharged by the gate operative at the landfill site. The duty of care stresses the responsibility of the producer but equally gives responsibility to the disposer. Traditionally the waste management industry has been seen as unprofessional but recent regulation and the growth of multinational waste companies has resulted in, among other things, greater scrutiny given to materials entering landfill sites and waste incineration facilities. This situation has arisen partly because the Environment Agency has increased inspection of waste management licensed sites.

This example of poor performance shows that environmental non-compliance need not result in prosecution but will result in additional costs to the producer in question. Careful planning and correct execution of compliant operations save valuable resources and, perhaps the most valuable resource, time.

Case Two – Reducing Waste for Customer and Supplier

Company B sought an opportunity to reduce both wasted time and resources arising from a traditional packaging process. The company produced reels of food and pharmaceutical grade packaging products. At goods-out transport packaging included stacking reels of printed stock onto wooden pallets and encasing it in plastic film and strapping down using steel banding all of which took time and purchased resources. The customer operated a form of just-in-time system which meant stock was put into the production process within a very short period of time of arrival.

Company B, a small company employing some 45 people, suggested to the customer, a FTSE 100 plc, that this process was wasteful. It cost B money to purchase the non-returnable packaging and the customer had the expense of disposing of the waste packaging. Further, it cost both companies valuable staff time to pack and unpack the product. Company B suggested that the introduction of robust returnable packaging would reduce both parties' costs. B invested in a fabricated returnable pallet.

The effect of this innovation – long before the current packaging regulations were even a twinkle in the European Commission's eye – was to reduce costs for both supplier and customer. The real benefit, however, was the additional contractual security offered to Company B by the innovation. Any competitor would need to identify and make similar investment and changes in order to be considered by that customer.

Case Three – Minimising Waste Contractor Risks

Company C operates from many small sites around the country, each retaining a local waste management contractor. Waste was generally not managed in compliance with the duty of care, for various reasons. C had contracts with some 80 different local contractors, many of them small and unprofessionally run, but cheap. A review of suppliers showed that this practice posed an unacceptably high risk of environmental non-compliance. Action was taken to reduce the number of companies with contracts for waste management with C down to only two. This action resulted in greater control, reduced risk of non-compliance and more efficient administration of the contracts. The commercial argument is unambiguous. The reason that so many contractors had been retained was primarily due to the payment conditions imposed by C on its contractors. By guaranteeing long-term, large-scale contracts, C could impose its payment conditions on larger, more reputable and lower risk waste management companies.

Why had this action not been taken before? Lack of clear understanding of the risks of non-compliance and lethargy were probably the primary factors. The commercial benefits to Company C are clear and set out above, but there is another important lesson to be learned by the 'unlucky' small waste companies that lost valuable contracts. This lesson should be learned by all in a contractual relationship with another company where there is an identified risk of environmental non-compliance. As the level of understanding of the commercial implications of environmental (non-)compliance increases in large businesses, so they will review their suppliers with a view to ceasing trading with those that pose an unacceptable risk. Thus, there is a commercial imperative on smaller businesses to improve their understanding of their own responsibilities and the responsibilities they take when entering into a contract with another party. If they do not, they need not fear prosecution but loss of business long before any appearance in court. A large company should not wait for its contractors to be prosecuted for they can eliminate the risk where any threat exists to their own security or public image by ceasing trading. 'Small *and ignorant* is *not* beautiful' (paraphrasing E. F. Schumacher, sorry) to a large environmentally aware business looking to eliminate risks of environmental non-compliance.

It is apparent from these examples, but particularly the third, that environmental compliance issues must be a mainstream part of business practices (*see* Chapter 5). Without due consideration and effective action, valuable resources will be wasted in vague and vain attempts to accept the challenge.

Producer Responsibility Obligations (Packaging Waste) Regulations 1997

The translation of the Packaging and Packaging Waste Directive into UK law has caused concern in many companies. There are opportunities for those companies which understand the implications of these regulations to their business. All regulations provide an opportunity both for those directly covered under the law and those not covered but with products or services which can be used to aid customers to comply with the legislation. As these are new regulations, a brief introduction and description follows and precedes the discussion on opportunities for companies seeking to benefit from compliance.

Background to the Regulations

The EU developed directive 94/62/EC in response to the growing concern for the quantity of packaging waste material being produced. The life of a piece of packaging is generally short and ends up generally in a landfill. Thus the rationale for the directive was to introduce an obligation on Member States to encourage increased recovery and recycling of packaging and packaging waste materials.

The directive 94/62/EC includes all packaging and packaging waste in the European market. The deadline for implementation by Member States of the directive was 30th June 1996. Member States have to demonstrate how the following targets could be achieved:

* 50–65% by weight of packaging waste to be recovered;

* 25–45% by weight of this total to be recycled (a minimum of 15% by weight for each material category).

These directive targets apply to each Member State, not to any part of society within the Member State. The targets will be subject to review and to possible amendment every five years. Ireland, Portugal and Greece have been given an additional five years to produce the infrastructure necessary to allow compliance.

The UK's Producer Responsibility Obligations (Packaging Waste) Regulations were enacted on 6th March 1997 under sections 93–95 of the Environment Act 1995. The regulations aim to:

- achieve a more sustainable approach to dealing with packaging waste;

- reduce the amount of packaging waste deposited in landfill;

- implement the recovery and recycling targets in the EC Directive on Packaging and Packaging Waste (94/62/EC);

- respond to UK industry's wish to have legislation to deter 'free-riders', business-led collective schemes to discharge businesses' obligations for them, and an approach which shares the recovery and recycling obligation between all parts of the packaging chain.

It is this final aim which distinguishes the UK response from that in other Member States, and has created complex regulations. It is worth noting, however, that Ireland has chosen to adopt a very similar approach to the UK, so perhaps we do not learn effectively from other's mistakes.

Producer Obligations

Not all businesses will be affected by the regulations. An obligated company must be a producer, who is a legal person who:

- performs an activity; **and**

- supplies packaging which he owns (holds legal title to) to another stage in the packaging chain where an activity will be performed or to the final user of the packaging.

A series of threshold tests are used to determine whether a producer has an obligation. These tests should be annually reviewed as producers may fall out of the scope of the regulations at any point –

especially if the company changes manufacturing practices and reduces the amount of obligated packaging handled in a calendar year.

A producer must satisfy the conditions of **both** threshold tests:

- producers with a turnover in excess of £5 million (or £1 m after 1st January 2000) for the last financial year for which audited accounts are available;

- producers that handled more than 50 tonnes of packaging and packaging materials in the previous calendar year.

Having determined whether or not a company is a producer and that it exceeds the test thresholds it then has three main obligations:

- **Registration obligation**, including data on packaging amounts – registration is required by 1st April annually with either the Environment Agency or the Scottish Environment Protection Agency, depending upon the location of the principal place of business.

- **Recovery and recycling obligation** – beginning in 1998, producers must take *reasonable steps* to recover and recycle specific tonnage of packaging waste calculated using three factors:

  - the tonnage of packaging handled by the producer in the previous calendar year;

  - the percentage obligation of the shared approach for each of the activities performed by the producer;

  - the national recovery and recycling targets.

- **Certifying obligation** – an 'approved person' (Regulation 23) must certify that the producer has discharged its recovery and recycling obligations based on the previous year's tonnage by 31st January in the year following the relevant period.

Compliance Options

Obligated companies have a choice from two options to comply with the regulations: make individual arrangements to comply with the legal obligations (going it alone); or join a registered compliance scheme.

Going it alone

The individual route means that a company must:

- consider whether it is a producer and has obligations under the regulations as described above.

- register with the Environment Agency (England and Wales) or SEPA (Scotland), pay an annual registration fee of £750, and complete the Agencies' data form based on the amount of packaging handled in the previous year. This process must be completed by 1st April annually.

- calculate the tonnage of packaging waste that it must recover and recycle by the end of 1998.

- confirm that specified tonnage has been recovered and recycled by 31st January the following year.

This process will require some resources in terms of staff time and an understanding of the internal processes involved. A company which chooses individual compliance should consider, before deciding on this option, exactly how it intends to comply. Even simple cost-benefit analysis is difficult at present because of the uncertainty over the price of compliance. Companies must be aware of the need to negotiate prices and enter into contracts with reprocessors as appropriate.

At this stage the company should consider the following:

- the nature of the obligation it has, e.g. the amount and complexity of the materials which make up its handled packaging;

- the internal systems already in place to recover and recycle packaging waste;

- the costs of joining a compliance scheme;

- the relationship it has at present with reprocessors.

Joining a Compliance Scheme

Under Regulation 4 producers joining a scheme will be exempt from their legal obligations if the following conditions are satisfied:

- the compliance scheme successfully discharges the obligations of its members;

- the company complies with the conditions of membership of the scheme in question.

There is a growing number of schemes to choose from in the UK. Unlike in other EU Member States competition was considered to be essential and, as of March 1998, there were eight registered and approved schemes with a further five awaiting confirmation of their status. The schemes vary in their exact structure but essentially provide a mechanism whereby Packaging Recovery Notes can be purchased in bulk. Considerable uncertainty still exists as to the exact nature and success of the schemes on offer. There are some issues which need to be addressed when considering which scheme to join.

- In most cases the producer company must provide data to the scheme – in some cases these data are checked by the scheme or agents of the scheme – in advance of the 1st April deadline. Therefore, when considering schemes, the internal resource commitment must be planned into the process of packaging compliance.

- Only three schemes have publicly stated what price the PRN is likely to be for members.

- Some schemes are owned by leading waste management companies because of the access they have to packaging waste materials and this might be a negative for some companies which fear a 'hard-sell' approach.

Benefiting from the Packaging Regulations

With this basic information in front of us, it should now be possible to address the emerging opportunities and to look at some specific cases.

- **Waste Management Practice.** The Packaging Regulations have an impact on the process, production and management of waste. For example, segregation and reclamation of back-door transit packaging waste can be sent for recycling and credits gained. But the process needs to be thought through carefully, especially if individual compliance is the chosen route as the onus is on the producer to provide evidence and demonstrate its accuracy in order to discharge the certification obligation.

- **Redesigning Packaging and Using Life-cycle Analysis Techniques.** Opportunities exist in complying with – or indeed avoiding – the regulations by redesigning and reviewing the nature or necessity of some packaging. For example, if a company is operating close to the 50 tonne threshold, it might choose to exploit the opportunity to reduce packaging handled to below that threshold. This could be achieved by:

  - the introduction of re-usable packaging which can take out of the calculation a large weight of unnecessary packaging;

  - reducing the weight of individual units of packaging;

  - reducing the layers or combinations of different packaging around the product.

  Further review of the life-cycle of your packaging products can show up areas of significant product or service improvement, which can be used in maintaining or obtaining a competitive advantage.

- **Supplier/Customer Requirements.** The processes in the packaging chain are interconnected and so actions at one point can/will have implications elsewhere. It is apparent that as the regulations currently stand there is an argument which suggests that if a producer can increase its own back-door waste then it can be used to discharge its recovery and recycling obligation – thus your customers could ask you to increase the amount of transit packaging you supply. This puts an increased burden on your obligations and so on back up the chain. But the commercial sense in this is missing – it is viewing the packaging regulations as the only factor in the decision-making process, which is clearly not the case. But all parties can benefit if packaging and packaging waste can be reduced or reused (*see* Case Two above).

Local Air Quality Regulations

Many companies have obligations under Part I of the Environmental Protection Act requiring those operating processes that emit substances into the air to register with the local authority (so called Part B processes). This system sets standards of emissions and through the principle of best available techniques not entailing excessive cost (BATNEEC) companies must improve their performance over a period of time.

Case Study Four – Registering an Existing Process

Company D was operating a prescribed process involving the burning of waste oil in large heating boilers. The process has been used in this particular industry as an effective method of using recovered oils to generate heat and thus use less bought in fuel oils. The environmental benefits are twofold: less waste oil being taken off site and disposed of and less oil purchased to generate heat. In this case it was estimated that the re-using of oil for burning saved about £20,000 per annum. The process had not been authorised under the regulations governing the burning of such oils. After review a recommendation was made to register the process. The process was beyond the deadline for authorisation (31 January 1996) and therefore there was a serious risk of prosecution upon discovery. Although outside the deadline the company contacted the local authority responsible for the area and the process – informing them that the company had now been advised that this process needed authorisation. The local environmental health officer was sympathetic and advised the company what was required and assisted in the application and authorisation process. Technically the company should have been penalised for failure to meet the legal timetable. A number of reasons might be suggested as to why the local authority treated the matter leniently.

•   Company D had recognised the problem and openly admitted fault.

- The company had not operated the process in a poor manner – it had merely not authorised it as required by the EPA90.

- The company was operating a process that re-used materials, which otherwise would become waste and saved a significant sum of money as a result.

- The local authority was happy to receive the application fee for the process and to be involved early on.

- The local authority would have seen little benefit in prosecuting Company D.

Case Study Five – Improving an Existing Process

An authorisation to operate an existing prescribed process contains a requirement to upgrade the process to meet BATNEEC. BATNEEC for each process is described within the relevant guidance notes, issued and reviewed under provisions set out in Part I of the Environmental Protection Act 1990. The procedure for improvement is usually agreed between the operator of the process and the relevant regulator. Problems can occur, however, when neither side takes a particularly strong lead in this procedure. Fear of the unknown is often the barrier for the operator and lack of time or human resource can be the barriers for the regulator. It is necessary to emphasise at this stage that it is the responsibility of the operator to apply for and manage the process – after all the operator carries the liabilities of breaching an authorisation or being discovered operating a process without an authorisation.

Company E was operating a Part B prescribed process with an authorisation from its local authority environmental health department. Both parties knew, however, that the annual monitoring records for volatile organic compounds (VOCs) showed levels that exceeded the limits set down in the official guidance and in the authorisation. The local authority did not act positively by issuing a prohibition notice; the reason why was not apparent. The company was prepared to accept this state of affairs because it could continue to operate the process without significant further investment to reduce the concentration of the emissions to meet the authorised levels. What led the company to take the lead was that this state of affairs was identified as a major problem during an audit. The company was at risk because the basic ground rules of the relationship between regulator and regulated were unclear and while in the past no problems had existed there was no guarantee that the situation would remain the same. After consultation with the local authority, a plan was agreed that meant the concentration of VOC was to be reduced to an acceptable level. If the plan did not deliver the improvement in performance then the authority would issue a prohibition notice. Why should Company E place itself in such a potentially threatened position? The reasons are complex, but can be described simply. Operating with an authorisation is, in effect, a licence to pollute. Operating outside the conditions of that authorisation produces a risk of prohibition and ultimately prosecution. Operating within limits provides a degree of commercial certainty – which cannot immediately and simply be quantified. A cost–benefit analysis can be performed based on the premise that if the process cannot be operated within its limits without major investment, then the alternative is to contract out the work to another company. This brings additional cost and lack of control. Further investigation showed that opportunities existed if steps were taken to recover the VOC vapour and return it for re-use.

As a result Company E meets the conditions of the authorisation, retains control of a critical part of its business, minimises the risk of enforced closure of the process and reduces the raw materials costs. Why has none of this been done before? The reasons seem to be partly a lack of confidence on the part of the company to take the lead, and partly because management attention had not been focused on this issue since the installation of the plant. Each party gained – the local authority now has a process operating with emission concentrations below one twentieth the previous level and the company gained for the reasons stated above.

Statutory Nuisance

Part III of the Environmental Protection Act 1990 introduces into law a criminal offence if a nuisance is judged to have been caused. Statutory nuisance covers activities that give rise to:

- dangerous premises;

- smoke, fumes or gases;

- dust, steam, smell or other effluviant;

- any accumulation or deposit;

- noise.

Nuisances are often exposed when a neighbour complains to the local authority about an activity. Noise nuisance is becoming more common, especially as local communities are increasingly aware of the legal options. Industry must be aware of any activities with the potential to become a nuisance and take steps to address the cause. This is best achieved by undertaking regular risk assessments (see below – accident prevention in the section on water pollution and environmental risk assessment in Chapter 3).

The frequency and nature of complaints that might result in proceedings are a function of the structure of the local community. This structure needs to be taken into account when assessing the potential risk. Hospitals and schools can be described as high-risk neighbours which are more sensitive to the causes of nuisance listed above. Local housing may vary in sensitivity, variation being dependent on the interaction of the occupants with the local business. As a general rule, a company can expect more complaints from a community of people who do not work in the business. They are less likely to complain about poor performance when the local people rely on a business for employment and salary.

Case Study Six – Dark Smoke

Company F caused a nuisance by emitting dark smoke containing coal dust from a steam-raising boiler. After prolonged and substantiated complaints by the local residents, the local authority took action. The company was taken to court after failing to solve the problem after the local authority had issued a notice. The cause of the problem was eventually traced to substandard coal supplied for use in the boiler. The boiler had worked satisfactorily when the required standard of coal was used. The coal merchant had switched to a different grade of coal – for reasons I shall leave to the reader's imagination – and the switch had remained undetected throughout the period of the notice. After changing supplier and grade of coal the problem was solved satisfactorily.

A number of issues are raised by this case study. First, Company F should have taken greater care in supervising the grade of coal used in the boiler, especially after the first occurrence of complaints. Sometimes complaints are ignored until a sufficient number has been received. A company should have an effective procedure to investigate the causes of any complaint. Secondly, the local community should have been kept informed of the process undertaken by the company to identify and solve the problem. Often this type of action can 'buy time' for a company to reach a satisfactory conclusion for each party.

Contaminated Land

Many companies are becoming concerned with contaminated land, particularly those subject to acquisition, those seeking investment from banks and those which have outgrown existing sites. The current and likely future policy in UK is to encourage the development of brownfield sites and to discourage encroachment into greenfield areas. This policy has already seen greater attention on the part of developers to the nature of the land and the potential for substances in, on or under that land to cause pollution. Legislation has been drafted but as yet has not been enacted in Part IIA of the Environmental Protection Act 1990. The so-called Contaminated Land Regime uses a simple risk-based approach to assessing whether land should be described as contaminated and therefore requires some form of remediation. Some local authorities are already using the guidance in deciding on planning conditions for new developments. The view, informally expressed, is that with guidance in existence, all involved in development should enter into the process of developing 'brown' land with a clear understanding of the potential for retrospective liabilities. They argue that local authorities would be failing if they do not address contamination and its remediation up front.

Even though the legislation is not enacted (at the time of going to press), it would be prudent for any company to use the methodology contained in the guidance when it has or believes that it has contaminated land. The approach contained in draft versions of the guidance issued for Part IIA is a simple and replicable technique for assessing the risk by identifying the source of potential contamination, the pathway and target. The benefit of the approach is that a better understanding of the situation can lead to more cost-effective remediation – or no requirement to remediate at all. Figure 2.2 shows the source, pathway and target basis for assessing and remediating contamination. Dig and dump is the conventional approach to dealing with contaminated land, which focused attention on the source. It is an expensive technique which does not always address the risk presented to the environment of the contaminants in the land – as the waste contaminant is merely transferred to a landfill.

Figure 2.2 Source, Pathway, Target

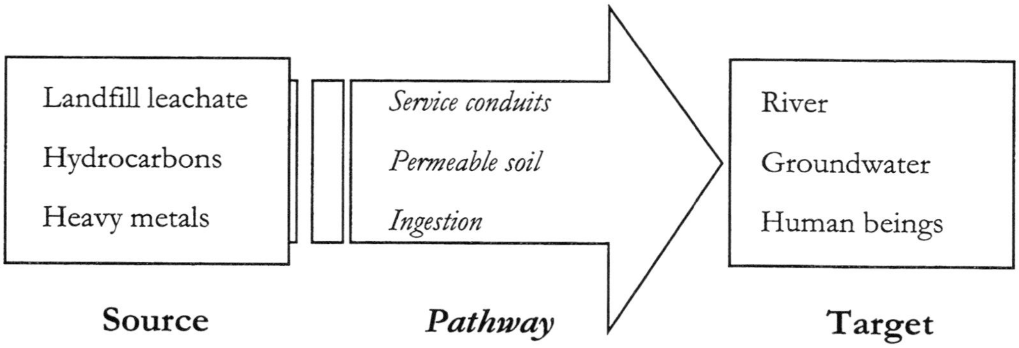

Landfill leachate	*Service conduits*	River
Hydrocarbons	*Permeable soil*	Groundwater
Heavy metals	*Ingestion*	Human beings
Source	*Pathway*	**Target**

Water Pollution

The general public sees water pollution often as the most important local environmental issue. Discharging waste substances to the aquatic environment has been standard practice for many businesses since the earliest times. In fact, the ability to discharge waste cheaply has been used as a principal factor in locating a factory. But changes in the law and public perception have led business to review this practice. As with other aspects of waste management, there are commercial benefits for those businesses which reduce the amount of wastewater they discharge. Figure 2.3 shows the relationship between charging for both supply and discharge on a standard metered water bill.

Causing or Knowingly Permitting

The principle of compliance applies to water and wastewater, namely knowledge of the process and the application of the relevant laws. The law controlling substances which can be discharged into rivers and sewers was revised in the early 1990s. Fundamentally, an offence is created if a person 'causes or

Figure 2.3 The Cost of Water from Mains through Process to Sewer Discharge

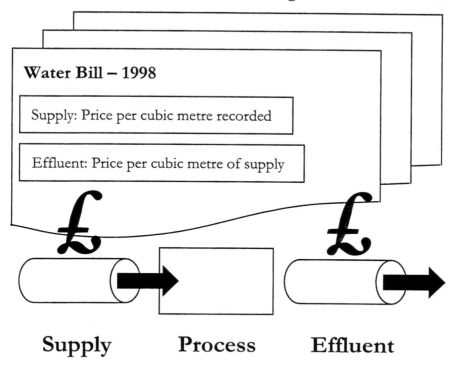

knowingly permits' pollution as a result of a discharge to water or to sewers. A permit or consent may be obtained to enable an operator to discharge effluent containing polluting matter. The consent contains limits on stated parameters or characteristics for the discharge. Discovery of a failure to comply may result in the serving of a notice prohibiting the continuation of the discharge. The method of calculating the concentration of substances in the effluent is based on a mass flow. The equation takes account of flow in the receiving water and the concentration of the effluent. Effluent composition is not simple and the consented concentrations of the pollutants must reflect their physico-chemical and biological characteristics. Some pollutants, such as chloride, are conservative and others react in the water environment. The actual permitted concentration of pollutants varies from place to place and from time to time. It is, therefore, in the interest of the company to understand the nature of the pollutants. Effluent parameters most often included in a consent, either to controlled water or sewer, are suspended solids, biochemical oxygen demand (BOD), ammonia, pH and temperature, with metals and organic substances as relevant to the particular discharge. Further reading is offered for greater detail on this regulatory issue.

Conservation and Increased Risk of Non-compliance

Water conservation can produce clear commercial and environmental benefits. The direct relationship between supply cost and discharge cost (Figure 2.3) makes conservation doubly effective. Water conservation must, however, be undertaken carefully because of the legal framework covering control of pollution. Table 2.1 contains an example of the challenge which can be presented in the event of successful conservation measures when no change occurs in the nature of the effluent. If volume is reduced using established good practice measures without alteration to the amount of pollutant, then there is an increased risk of failure to keep within the limits of the consent. Conservation may, therefore, present commercial benefits but increase legal liability.

Table 2.1 Water Conservation and Increased Legal Risk

Parameter	Consented limit	Average pre-conservation level	After conservation
Volume (m³ week⁻¹)	300	200	100
BOD (mg l⁻¹)	300	200	400
Suspended solids (mg l⁻¹)	250	200	400

Accidental Water Pollution

Discharges can occur in an unplanned and uncontrolled manner. Accidents can lead to unforeseen pollution of water, but the legal liability remains with the person causing the pollution. This feature of environmental legislation can be demonstrated in a number ways. Prosecution can result from the following incidents:

* oil leaking from poorly maintained storage facilities;

* soil wash-off from exposed surfaces;

- road or rail freight accidents;

- runoff of contaminated fire-fighting water;

- seepage of dissolved substances in land contaminated from past activities;

- vandalism.

Accidents present, perhaps, the greatest risk to the water environment because of the instantaneous impact of pollutants on aquatic ecosystems. Environment Agency (and National Rivers Authority before April 1996) figures show that the agriculture and construction sectors are consistently the most frequently prosecuted for water pollution. Many of the incidents in these sectors can be classed as accidental. Lack of awareness and preparedness can be identified in many cases as the primary cause of such incidents – but may not be a defence for the accidental polluter.

Accident Prevention

Risk assessment can be a valuable tool in minimising the occurrence of accidents resulting in pollution of the water environment. Simple assessment techniques can be used to identify high-risk areas of activity and lead to improvement of prevention and control measures. It is not necessary to use sophisticated risk assessment with detailed analysis of probabilities. It is, however, necessary to follow some simple rules if the process is to be effective in preventing pollution:

- Use standard techniques when appropriate – e.g. Operator Pollution Risk Appraisal (OPRA) introduced for IPC process operators by HMIP (now carried on by the Environment Agency).

- Repeat the process regularly to ensure that the hazard has not changed and that prevention measures are still sufficient.

- Ensure that people undertaking risk assessments are competent and do not have a vested interest in the activity.

Table 2.2 shows some of the mitigation measures suitable for incidents which can create accidental pollution listed above. It is often the case that only one measure is used, but risk may remain relatively high unless mitigation measures are adopted in series. Mitigation measures only reduce the risk of causing pollution; they do not provide any added value, which can be created if steps are taken to prevent pollution in the first place. Pollution risk prevention can be achieved only by removing the hazard; this is often not a practicable option.

Table 2.2 Accidental Water Pollution Risk Reduction

Hazard	Pollution risk reduction measure
Oil and other environmentally hazardous substances leaking from unfit-for-purpose storage	Well-maintained bunding of adequate volume Bulk storage above ground Oil spillage kits adjacent to storage areas
Soil wash-off from exposed surfaces	Geotextile covering Runoff and sediment collection lagoons
Road or rail freight accidents	Emergency procedure incorporating rapid response clean-up
Runoff of contaminated fire-fighting water	Fire-fighting water retention
Seepage of dissolved substances in land contaminated from past activities	Site investigation Cut pathway between source and target (*see* Figure 2.2)
Vandalism	Site security to address potential problem – i.e. disaffected staff or external public access

Cost will always be an issue in determining which option, if any, is used, but the benefit of reducing the risk of prosecution should be included in the determination of cost–benefit. Water conservation can produce cost savings but preventing water pollution produces cost avoidance – which can be difficult or impossible to quantify accurately.

Gaining Benefits from Complying with Future Legislation

Businesses need to look beyond the requirements of present legislation if they wish to gain continued benefits. A business which only addresses new legislation after it has been introduced exposes itself to unplanned activity and the concurrent risk of financial over-exposure. There is one major piece of new legislation which is set to change environmental protection legislation throughout the European Union. The directive on integrated pollution prevention and control will change the way that some 15,000 businesses in the UK are regulated.

The IPPC Directive

The EU directive on integrated pollution prevention and control (IPPC) was passed on 24th September 1996. It has introduced a timetable which over the next 10 years will see more and more diverse industrial and commercial processes and activities being regulated in a manner similar to that already in place through the IPC regime in Part I of the Environmental Protection Act 1990.

The purpose of the directive is to achieve integrated pollution prevention and control of a list of activities specified in Annex I to the directive. On the whole these are similar to the list of prescribed processes under the IPC regime set out by Part I of the Environmental Protection Act 1990. There are, however, some significant differences between the IPC regime and the directive which will extend the scope and extent of impact on regulated industries.

Timing

The directive came into force on 31st October 1996 and must be adopted by Member States through the introduction or amendment of legislation to comply with it within three years of that date.

It will apply to 'new installations' from 30th October 1999 and must be applied to all 'existing installations' by October 2007. The definition of 'existing installations' includes not only those which are already in operation, but also those which have been authorised or have been subject to a full request for authorisation by 30th October 1999, in the view of the relevant regulatory authority.

Scope of the Directive

Article 3 of the directive lays down certain principles which Member States must ensure are applied by their regulatory authorities in relation to installations carrying out relevant activities. The regulatory authorities can comply by taking these principles into account when determining the conditions to be attached to the operating permits that the directive requires all installations to be subject to. The principles are:

- all appropriate preventative measures against pollution must be taken, in particular through the application of the best available techniques (BAT);

- no significant pollution must be caused;

- waste production must be avoided in accordance with the waste framework directive, or where produced must be recovered, or where that is 'technically and economically impossible', waste must be disposed of in a manner that avoids or reduces any impact on the environment;

- energy must be used efficiently;

- necessary measures must be taken to prevent accidents and limit their consequences;

- necessary measures must be taken upon cessation of the activities to avoid any pollution risk and return the site to a 'satisfactory state'.

The BAT Concept

The concept of BAT plays a central role in the directive. Its objective is to provide a basis for emission limit values (ELVs). BAT provides the principal benchmark for determining the obligations of industrial operators in respect of pollution prevention and control. BAT is defined in the directive in terms of its component words:

- 'best' means 'most effective in achieving a high general level of protection of the environment as a whole';

- 'available' means 'developed on a scale which allows implementation in the relevant sector, under economically and technically viable conditions, taking into consideration the costs and advantages, whether or not the techniques are used or produced inside the Member State in question, as long as they are reasonably accessible to the operator'. This definition is carefully constructed to avoid the two extremes of, on the one hand, totally ignoring the cost and practical feasibility of applying a technique or, on the other hand, leaving competent authorities the possibility of considering only techniques used or developed locally;

- 'techniques' refers not only to the technology used but also to the way in which the installation is designed, built, maintained, operated and decommissioned. It is a wide term designed to include factors relevant to the environmental performance of an installation – such as environmental management systems and environmental risk assessment and audit.

Article 16, paragraph 2 of the IPPC directive requires the Commission to organise 'an exchange of information between Member States and the industries concerned on best available techniques, associated monitoring and developments in them', and to publish the results of the exchanges of information. The primary objective of such an exercise is to support the competent authorities in their implementation of the directive and, in particular, in their obligation to follow developments in BAT. In addition, the participation of industry and the general availability of the published results should in itself stimulate the uptake of cleaner production techniques.

The approach taken is sector by sector. The results of the information exchange will take the form of BAT Reference Documents (BREFs) and will be published for each of the about 30 sectors. BREFs are designed as a tool to assist competent authorities by giving practical guidance and information on what BAT means for a given sector. Although the contents of the BREFs – which include 'reference levels' for environmental performance such as numerical emission or consumption levels – will not have any legal status as binding provisions, they must be taken into consideration when determining BAT.

The first three draft BREFs are now available – and make little effective difference to our understanding of how IPPC will be implemented.

Differences between IPPC and IPC

The directive shows many of the features of the IPC regime, which is not surprising when we consider that the official who drafted the directive was on secondment from the Department of the Environment. Although much of the directive sounds familiar to those accustomed to the existing IPC regime, it is not difficult to compile a long list of differences which could have a substantial impact on business.

Extent of Control at the Installation

The directive controls pollution from 'activities', whereas IPC deals with 'processes'. If an activity listed in Annex I to the IPPC directive takes place at a particular site then 'any other directly associated activities which could have a technical connection with the activities carried out on that site and which could have an effect on emissions and pollution' will also be subject to IPPC. Under the existing IPC regime only the particular 'prescribed process' is subject to authorisation. This change in the extent of the regulation of emissions and pollution will have an effect on existing authorised processes in that on-site activities, which currently occur outside the process boundary and are not authorised, will need to be considered in light of the directive.

Coverage of Additional Activities

A number of activities, which are not subject to IPC, will be subject to IPPC permits under the directive, including:

• landfills receiving more than 10 tonnes per day of waste or with a capacity of more that 25,000 tonnes;

• installations for the intensive rearing of poultry and pigs; and

• food processing and treatment installations.

Wider Definition of Pollution

The directive defines 'pollution' as 'the direct or indirect introduction as a result of human activity, of substances, vibrations, heat or noise into the air, water or land which may be harmful to human health or the quality of the environment...' The definition given under IPC does not cover vibrations or noise.

Targeting All Emissions

The broader scope of IPPC described in the general principles (above) is also reflected in the aims of the IPPC system as stated in the directive. IPPC aims to prevent or reduce emissions to the environment, whereas IPC aims to prevent or reduce pollution of the environment. This may appear to be a semantic distinction of little consequence but it has fairly wide implications.

IPC in the UK has tended to mean looking at how to prevent or reduce pollution risk to the receiving environment in a manner which takes account of emissions to air, water and land. The IPPC approach moves well beyond this in stating that the aim is to reduce all emissions to the environment. 'Emissions' in the language of the directive are the direct and indirect release of substances (meaning any chemical element and its compounds), vibration, heat or noise.

Reducing all emissions involves looking not only at potentially harmful substances being discharged but also at reducing all discharges of any substances whether known to be harmful or not. It also involves reducing the amount of raw materials consumed and increasing the energy efficiency of the activity.

BAT and BATNEEC

The directive refers to the 'best available techniques' for preventing or reducing pollution, whereas the IPC regime refers to the 'best available techniques not entailing excessive cost'. The directive says that an assessment of BAT should include an assessment of 'costs and advantages', including the use of low waste technology, the use of less hazardous substances, the consumption and nature of raw materials (including water) and their energy efficiency.

An assessment of BATNEEC under IPC is not generally considered to extend beyond the costs of the industry concerned or affordability. However, the wording of the directive apparently confers discretion to consider not only costs and advantages to the activity being regulated but wider factors such as the effects on public health and the broader environment – in other words, to give higher priority to cost and benefit in decision-making criteria and reduced priority to affordability.

Additional Information Required in the Application

The application for a permit under the directive needs to include some information which is not specifically required under IPC. This is described in Table 2.3.

Table 2.3 Differences in Information Required in Applications

IPPC	IPC
Raw and auxiliary materials, other substances and energy used and generated	Prescribed substances and those with the potential to cause harm only
A description of the conditions of the site for the purpose of identifying past and future land contamination	Not required
The nature and quantities of foreseeable emissions from the installations	Emissions of prescribed substances which may cause harm
Measures for the prevention and recovery of waste	Not required
Measures to prevent accidents	Not required
Non-technical summary	Not required

Regulation of Accident Hazards

One of the basic requirements of Article 3 which will give rise to the need to provide information not required by IPC arises out of the requirement for regulatory authorities to ensure that installations are operated in a manner which prevents accidents.

In the UK the Control of Industrial Accident Hazards Regulations 1994 that are derived from the European Union's 1982 directive on the subject is the main vehicle for regulating such matters. The regulatory body is the Health and Safety Executive (HSE) rather than the Environment Agency and the operator is obliged to report on substances present at the site and the measures taken to ensure safe operation.

The directive does not say that all regulation of a relevant activity has to be performed by one regulatory body through a single permit, but this would appear to be convenient. Therefore, in the future, this system is likely to be reviewed. The EU has revised the 1982 'Seveso' directive and the interaction between the COMAH (96/82/EC) and IPPC directives appears to have been officially addressed, in that actions by an operator in compliance with each directive can be transferred to the other, or 'recycled' as stated in the consultation draft.

Matters which Must Be Specified in the Permit

The directive requires various matters to be specified in the permit which the IPC regime does not insist on, although in practice they are often specified. These include:

- emission limit values for all 'pollutants' likely to be emitted from installations in significant quantities;

- monitoring requirements;

- supply of data to the regulatory authority; and

- measures relating to conditions other than normal operating conditions.

Future Developments to Pollution Control Regulation

There are likely to be further changes to the regulatory framework in the UK as a result of the introduction of IPPC. It is apparent that recent developments in the passage of IPPC into UK law have shown that as little as possible will be changed. In the Queen's Speech of 24th November 1998, there was no mention of pollution prevention and control and so we thought that IPPC would be introduced 'through the back door' as statutory instruments under existing IPC regulations. But we now await the formalisation of the Pollution prevention and control bill, which will replace entirely Part 1 of the EPA90.

Changes will probably be needed to UK legislation to bring waste disposal within the ambit of IPC. At present the IPC regime specifically excludes consideration of waste disposal because this is dealt with separately under Part II of the Environmental Protection Act 1990. Now that the Environment Agency has regulatory powers for this part of the Act, it appears that the way is clear for a change.

The pressure on smaller businesses to address their environmental impact is set to increase, as it is likely that any emitting substances listed in Annex III to the directive will become subject to IPPC.

IPPC may provide the impetus to many businesses thinking about developing and implementing an environmental management system. The similarity in approach and scope between ISO14001/EMAS and IPC has been identified for some time, but IPPC provides an even stronger basis for systematic environmental management, especially with its references to site condition, energy, materials efficiency and monitoring. This may then reopen the self-regulation debate in the UK, both because the recognised systems and IPPC are very similar and because there is increased pressure on the regulatory bodies as a result of the increased number of installations now required to comply.

Preparing for New Legislation

Throughout this chapter I have looked at how existing and new legislation can challenge operational and management approaches. Inside an organisation change is managed in a variety of different ways with varying degrees of success. As already stated above, when legislation is presented through EU directives a period of more than three years exists in which an organisation can prepare for the changes necessary to comply with new regulations.

In practice, an organisation must address the process of change in respect to both the internal and the external (regulatory and others) issues which will provide the boundaries and, to a degree, affect the way that this process is managed. Figure 2.4 shows how developing a strategy for new legislation can be simply developed as it is dependant on two parameters – industry openness and regulatory competence.

Figure 2.4 A Model for Developing Strategy for Change in Response to New Legislation

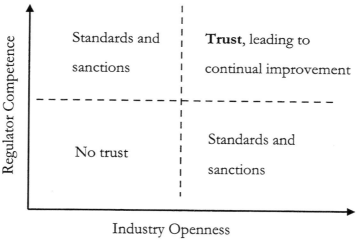

New legislation requires a level of regulator competence which can allow both parties to achieve desired goals. For the regulator the goal is to prevent pollution – therefore prosecutions may be seen as a failure. For industry the goal is to minimise the impact of new legislation, while gaining the benefits that are available. Effective legislation occurs when the regulated accept the central premise – for example murder is bad – thus a relationship can develop between various affected parties. Environmental legislation presents peculiar problems, in that the absolute criteria for what is pollution remain somewhat obscure. Therefore for industry to be open in dealings with the regulator they require assurance that the regulator is competent and can help in the process of achieving compliant status. This has not always been the case in the past.

If we work from Figure 2.4 and use the model to develop a strategy for change, then we can move towards a situation where trust and continual improvement exist, and where prosecution is truly the last resort after all else has failed. For the regulated to gain any potential long-term benefit, then trust must exist. To move from a position of no trust, both parties must accept partial responsibility to increase their understanding and become more open. Industry openness is chosen as the parameter because industry should be competent in understanding its own operations in light of the legislation but is often secretive. Secrecy is often a function of uncertainty and fear – neither can exist if trust is to develop.

If industry is to move from standards and sanctions to a position of mutual trust then either it must become more open or must assist the regulator to become more competent. When developing an appropriate strategy industry must first assess which box it is currently in. Once developed the strategy should then enable movement towards trust, continual improvement and the maximisation of benefits from new legislation.

A final note of caution is that the figure shows two dashed lines intersecting at a point. The location of this point is unknown and varies on a site by site and regulator to regulator basis. Just how open industry must be and how competent the regulator remain unanswered questions – ones that can only be answered in an iterative process of trial and error.

Summary

Statutory environmental compliance is a requirement of any responsible business. But gaining any commercial benefits can only be achieved if a company has a detailed knowledge of the relevant legislation and its application. The effectiveness of regulation is not an issue directly addressed in this book because it is dangerous to adopt a strategy that is based on the premise that low prosecution rates in the past will continue into the future. The responsibility rests with industry to comply with environmental legislation. The old adage – ignorance is no defence – applies in this and all areas of law. It is the duty of the regulated to educate itself and then take appropriate steps to ensure that the letter (and spirit, possibly) of the law are complied with at all times.

Strict liability as a central principle of UK environmental protection law needs to be understood by industry. When non-compliance occurs, it is our natural reaction to seek someone to blame for the failure. The law does not always make that distinction. If pollution occurs, and damage is caused and discovered, then the polluter will pay. We need to manage, through increased understanding, our activities to prevent pollution in the first place. Failure to do so may buy some time, but at some point in the future the hazard and risk will cause commercial problems. The methods of addressing risk are covered in greater detail in the next chapter.

CHAPTER 3

Non-Statutory Environmental Compliance

Introduction

As the range of stakeholders with an interest in an organisation's performance increases and each becomes more aware and sophisticated, so businesses need to adapt their approach to environmental compliance. The traditional focus on compliance with environmental protection legislation, without attention to broader requirements, needs to change. The concept of a two-phase system of where an organisation interacts is a simple method of visualising the interaction of different stakeholders in one place – for our purposes the company itself. Figure 3.1 sets out this two-phase approach. The vertical system represents the state of a business in Box A (Figure 1.1). As a business moves to consider the elements in the horizontal system, it moves into Box B. Without over-complicating what is a simple model, it is possible to suggest that in time some of the issues discussed in this chapter will extend the boundary of the vertical system out sideways to encompass more of the horizontal system components. The principal elements of ISO14001, for example, already encompass both vertical and horizontal systems within one management system.

What I shall call 'non-statutory' compliance encompasses a series of activities which need to adapt to the changing set of conditions which the two-phase approach shows to us. The principle of 'fundamental understanding prior to taking action' remains intact in this immature but growing area of environmental and strategic management and planning. Many of the activities covered in this chapter

Figure 3.1 A Two-Phase System for Environmental Compliance

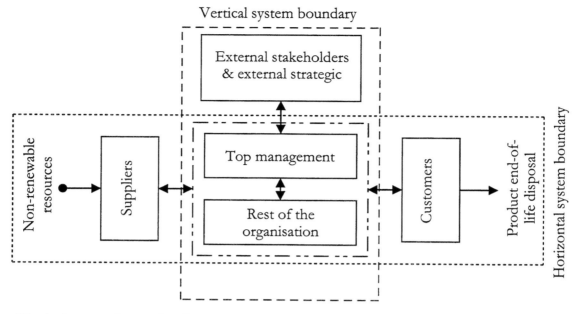

Vertical system is equal to Box A (Figure 1.1) and statutory compliance

emerge from a legal framework, but not exclusively and importantly not through a traditional normative method of environmental regulation. In short, others are increasingly setting the business agenda which in turn requires either compliance with criteria or standards set by a third party or compliance with internally (in terms of the organisation in question) set and agreed targets that allow improved performance as required by those third parties. In both cases the business benefit can only fully be realised with a comprehensive understanding of the way that internal activities interact with the external issues involved. It is not my intention to promote certified environmental management systems, but the inevitable linkage exists and should not be ignored. Broad compliance issues in such management systems are explored in Chapter 4.

Environmental Risk and Insurance

Environmental risk is constantly changing. The list of issues presented in Chapter 1 shows the range of risks is large and growing. As a priority, an organisation must review this dynamic set of commercial and societal concerns on a regular basis. Subsequently increasing numbers of companies then review the need to insure themselves against one-off or persistent environmental risks. The nature and extent of insurance cover will vary hugely, but one basic principle applies – the need for the insured to understand the commercial implications of the cover which is sought.

Insurance cover for environmental matters is becoming increasingly important as an issue for society in general and for business in particular. The basic challenge is to address the risk involved so that appropriate insurance cover can be provided at a cost to the insured which does not over expose the insurer. This is a complex area of financial and legal argument, which is comprehensively covered by Lockett (1996, – *see* Further reading).

The insurance industry would probably be the first to admit that risk analysis remains an inexact discipline. As further incidents and claims arise the insurance industry will be in a stronger position to provide appropriate cover based on a complex set of changing risks. As a statistical exercise, assessing risk for insurance purposes can be seen as a long-term, perhaps infinite experiment. The process of environmental risk analysis will be refined, but never truly completed. Take for example the risk of flooding from rivers or the sea.

The method of calculating the risk for a particular location is based on a complex set of factors, including the nature of the land-use, historical flooding frequency and magnitude, weather patterns at the location and the physical nature of the river catchment. In 1975 the Institute of Hydrology published a four-volume study of the rivers of England and Wales, called the Flood Studies Report (recently replaced with updated figures) which sets out the basis for assessing the risk of flooding. This form of environmental risk has been studied for many years. What is changing is the growing importance of a broader range of human interactions with the environment, most notably chemical substances in the environment, the impact of which is much more difficult to quantify than environmental issues such as river flooding.

Environmental Disasters

Lockett (1996) describes three types of disaster which result in environmental impacts. Each of these types requires a different assessment of risk and resulting insurance cover. All the disasters described are understood in principle but details of the risk are still relatively poorly defined.

Immediate Impact Disasters

These are generally either high profile disasters which have multinational impacts, or local disasters. High profile disasters such as *Exxon Valdez*, Chernobyl or Seveso are remote from everyday activities – but have real impacts on the environment and on the insurance industry. Local disasters such as Camelford or landfill gas migration are a real concern for the communities adjacent to the location of the incident.

Only some types of commercial activity are likely to experience this type of scale of disaster with immediate impact on the environment. As a very simple rule, activities which involve the transportation, handling and storage of large quantities of environmentally harmful substances need to be reviewed to determine the level and scope of cover to insure against losses and costs which may result.

Gradual Pollution Incidents

Love Canal is an excellent example of this type. Carcinogens released into the environment over the years prior to discovery in 1977 resulted in a $14 billion lawsuit. But other issues, such as asbestos clean-up, have raised longer-term concerns. As further exposure will result in more evidence to link health and environmental harm to gradual pollution from substances, so the risk analysis process will become more sophisticated.

This is apparently a very specific type of pollution incident, but any organisation which has a land holding, where that land may contain harmful substances, may become liable for the consequences at some point in the future.

Hybrid Disasters

These may be defined as pollution '*as a result of natural and man-made events where the effects of man-made operations interfere with the underlying biological functioning of nature*' (Lockett, 1996). The resulting long-term

Environmental Compliance   Non-Statutory Environmental Compliance

impacts have as yet uncalculated (perhaps incalculable) costs because of the complex interaction between pollutants and natural systems and further interaction between modified substances and natural systems. To place this in some context the EU currently estimate that 63,000 chemical substances are emitted into the environment; each will impact to some degree but will also interact to produce new unknown impacts.

Examples of hybrid disasters include:

- acid rain;

- heavy metal contamination of the food chain;

- impacts of over-extraction from ground water bodies; and

- genetic modification of organisms.

The long-term effects of pollution may arise out of the cumulative effects of short-lived episodes. For example, a seasonal feature of traffic pollution is high levels of ozone, to which is attributed the aggravation of lung and breathing disorders. Yet the ozone itself is not a substance emitted from vehicle exhausts but is a secondary pollutant created as a result of photochemical processes interrupting the rapid nitrogen cycle at a local scale (*see* Figure 3.2). Hybrid disasters of this sort present peculiar problems for insurers and the insured.

Figure 3.2 Simplified Process of Ozone Production in Urban Areas

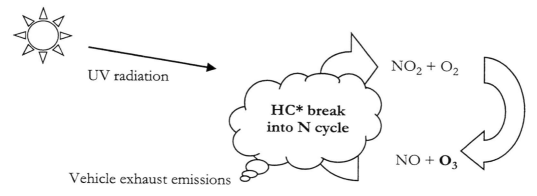

Organisational Issues in Risk and Insurance

Insurance cover beyond that for the immediate impact of environmental disasters will only be available to organisations with sophisticated, comprehensive loss control, risk analysis and management techniques. Consideration must therefore be given to disaster recovery, comprehensive loss control and risk management techniques. Attention must be given to planning and comprehensive reviews of management practices. This process requires a fundamental rethink of the level of management skills and techniques used in organisations. It is apparent that past attitudes, which can be expressed as either 'head in the sand' or 'no news is good news' is no longer applicable. Insurers are becoming increasingly aware of the complexities and until risk analysis can be improved to keep pace, the onus must be on the insured to understand as fully as possible the actual and potential risks involved. If they do not, then they are likely to be paying for premiums against loss which is next to impossible or are not satisfactorily covered for losses against everyday occurrences.

Insurers are involved in a process of assessing risk in a constantly changing set of circumstances. Risk management in an organisation must operate as an iterative process if liabilities are to continue to receive appropriate levels of cover. As the regulatory framework extends and changes focus to encompass retrospective liability both insured and insurers must review these procedures. At present it is perhaps easy to say that generally both insurer and insured are poorly prepared to respond adequately to the rapid changes in a range of issues.

Environmental Risk Assessment

Environmental risk assessment is an emerging discipline – emerging because we still cannot quantify precisely the consequence of a hazard. For many companies it is not financially feasible or commercially viable to undertake detailed and properly quantified risk analysis. This does not mean that nothing can be done to evaluate environmental risk. A term – which I prefer – that is increasingly used is 'risk estimation'. Without properly established, quantified and statistically significant probabilities, an organisation must use a technique to estimate risk that relies on a degree of subjectivity. It is fundamental for any assessment or estimation of risk to repeat or iterate the process, refining the technique as circumstances change.

As a result of a risk assessment an organisation can give, either internally or externally, reassurance that 'risky' activities are subjected to appropriate management or technical controls. To achieve this the risk estimation process must be carefully thought out and, most importantly, be documented and repeatable, however subjective the technique.

Hazard Identification

The first stage of risk assessment is to identify the hazards requiring control. These may relate to the issues covered in Chapter 2 such as waste disposal, water pollution and air pollution. The hazard should be carefully (and simply) described to reflect the precise nature of the activities being performed.

A hazard may be described as a property, activity or circumstance which has the potential to give rise to harm to the environment or human health, for example CFC use and disposal and bulk oil storage. Hazard identification must take account of all operational phases of the activities performed. At this stage no attempt should be made to assess the relative significance of the hazards – this follows in the stages of the assessment process.

Identifying Consequences

The consequences of the hazard need now to be classified to allow initial differentiation between those which are immediate impact disasters and those which are gradual pollution or hybrid disasters, for example (see above). The Contaminated Land Regime (described in Chapter 2) sets out a risk-based approach – and to attempt to standardise terminology – target and consequence are synonymous. There are no prescribed rules for this and the chosen methodology should suit the organisation's commercial and environmental concerns.

Research should be undertaken to estimate the consequences. This research does not have to be primary in nature but does need to take into account available scientific or policy information. Consequences depend on the combination of hazard and the characteristics of the receptor environment. In this way the same activity performed close to a neighbouring residential property or in a remote location will have very different consequences (*see* for example statutory nuisance in Chapter 2).

Estimation of Probability (Likelihood) of Consequences

This stage in risk evaluation is prone to the greatest subjectivity – hence the inclusion of the term of likelihood in parentheses in the above title. In practice it is not practicable to quantify the statistical probability of the realisation of the consequences of a hazard. Insurance companies do attempt to calculate the numerical probability of risk but the majority of industrial companies do not have the resources to produce such exact analysis. Indeed it is not always a good use of resources, because with a degree of expertise and a standardised approach similar answers will result from a simpler, subjective estimation.

An event which is likely to occur requires higher priority for management or technical control of the hazard. Conversely, an event which is unlikely (though not impossible) may not require such immediate action. A simple technique to describe likelihood is to use semi-quantitative ranges to distinguish between 'high', 'medium', 'low' and 'negligible'. If such an approach is used then clear guidance must be given to assessors to avoid 'operator' error in the process of assessing likelihood.

Estimating Environmental Risk

Risk can now be determined for each identified hazard, based on the nature or severity of the consequence and its likelihood (*see* Table 3.1). Matrices are a very simple method of estimating the resulting risk and thus directing the priority and nature of the management or technical controls or improvement. Such an approach should not be described as true risk evaluation, but it does provide a useful and pragmatic management tool which, if used properly and repeated periodically, can result in environmental risk reduction.

Table 3.1 Example of Risk Estimation Based on Magnitude
and Likelihood of Consequences

Likelihood or probability	Consequence			
	Severe	*Moderate*	*Mild*	*Negligible*
High	High	High	Medium/low	Near zero
Medium	High	Medium	Low	Near zero
Low	High/Medium	Medium/Low	Low	Near zero
Negligible	High/Medium/Low	Medium/Low	Low	Near zero

Operator and Pollution Risk Appraisal – An Example of Risk Assessment in Practice

The regulation of prescribed processes under Part I of the Environmental Protection Act 1990 has proved to be costly, time-consuming and prone to subjectivity. Her Majesty's Inspectorate of Pollution identified this and produced a practical and pragmatic method of assessing performance within these processes. By using a standard procedure of assessing the environmental risk presented by the process and its operation HMIP could prioritise its efforts. Operator and Pollution Risk Appraisal (OPRA) relates day-to-day management practices with the requirements of the process authorisation in an objective and consistent manner.

The OPRA rating results from the combination of two separate assessments:

•   operator performance appraisal, which includes:

     –   recording and use of information;

     –   knowledge and implementation of authorisation;

     –   plant maintenance;

- management and training;

- process operation;

- incidents, complaints and non-compliance events;

- recognised environmental management systems.

- pollution hazard appraisal:

  - presence of hazardous substances;

  - scale of hazardous substances;

  - frequency and nature of hazardous operations;

  - technologies for hazard abatement;

  - location of process;

  - offensive characteristics.

It is simple to see the application of the principles of risk appraisal. The Environment Agency produced a second edition of OPRA in 1997 and it is now in use throughout many of the authorised industry sectors. Such a simple method can be applied elsewhere and can be adapted to local operational considerations. The value of the method is that it presents a readily applicable process for setting objectives for improvements and strategy.

Environmental Risk Management

With a better estimation of risk it is now beholden on a company to address the highest risk activities. This can result in a variety of approaches including: management controls, technological improvements and/or insurance cover. The last option should not be considered to be an excuse to do nothing else – it is frequently a condition of insurance cover that one or both of the other approaches must be used in conjunction with the safeguard of insurance – and not to do so invalidates the cover.

Risk management is an integral part of the risk assessment process. This can be best explained using a simple example.

A large fuel storage facility is bunded to control the consequences of the hazard presented by the quantity of the substance contained. The management of the hazard is achieved by regular inspection and reporting of the competence of the bund wall to retain the content of the tanks. If at some point in the future the bund cracks or is damaged then the likelihood of the consequence will change from negligible to high. If the nature of the substance contained in the tanks changes then the consequence might be reduced from high to low.

It is simple to see that over time each element of the risk estimation process can change, in either a positive or negative direction. Each change must be reflected, if indeed it results in a new evaluation of the risk, in the nature of the management or technical controls used. All may have a direct impact on compliance with relevant conditions in insurance policies. Risk estimation provides a method of understanding and simplifying an extremely complex set of inter-related commercial, operational and environmental issues, thereby allowing effective risk management to be adopted.

Retrospective Environmental Liability

Further legal changes are ongoing in the UK, following the example from the USA, which will lead to the imposition of retrospective environmental liability. These changes will create a new challenge for insurers and the insured. There has tended to be reluctance on the part of both to address past environmental issues and the resultant liabilities. In the past governments have picked up these liabilities, but increasingly this is changing because of the growing realisation of the actual remedial costs involved. This change will be realised when Part IIA of the Environmental Protection Act 1990 becomes law (*see* Chapter 2). In reality many local authorities already have taken on the principles of retrospective liability when land is being developed.

Criteria for Risk Rating

Risk rating is a process of ranking the type of threat and thus helps in prioritising investment decisions. There are three main criteria in risk rating:

- environmental activities and risks with the potential to threaten the continued profitability or existence of an organisation such as: activities which threaten existing licences or those which have been applied for, activities which result in prosecution or imprisonment of directors, activities which result in the prohibition of core business functions;

- environmental activities and risks which reduce the value of assets such as property or products;

- environmental activities and risks which have the potential to lead to third-party damage or claims such as clean-up.

Lender Liability

In the USA, lender liability has become a serious consideration which previously was neglected. Most of the major banks in the UK now recognise this factor in the process of assessment prior to lending. The disclosure of environmental information to the financial services sector has become commonplace. Formal reporting has tended to gloss over or ignore environmental risk and resulting liabilities, although the reporting of environmental performance has become a marketing or communication tool. Environmental reporting will be covered in more detail later in this chapter.

Lender liability results when a company ceases to exist and the creditors take control of the assets of the failed business. The lender must therefore undertake a simple risk assessment of the business in question prior to entering into the contract. The bank is the lender to which most businesses turn to first. Many leading banks now have quite extensive assessment methodologies for so-called 'non-financial' risks, such as health and safety, employment practices and the environment. Each of these areas may have medium to long-term financial liabilities attached for a particular business and their lender. But it remains the case that, for most businesses, the loan only covers a short period and therefore the exposure of the lender to environmental risk is small. One leading bank has guidance on environmental risk for its business customer managers extending to over 100 pages, which in practice is rarely used for its intended purpose.

Assessment of environmental risk by lenders relies heavily on the 'gut' instinct of the banks' staff. In practice, the market is so competitive in other areas of lending that a bank will effectively ignore the risk, which can be quite large. It remains the case that environmental incidents are rare and therefore the calculated risk is small – small enough to be ignored by lenders.

Directors' and Officers' Liability

A company is a separate legal entity to be viewed in law as completely separate from its shareholders, members and officers and management. The management of the company rests with controlling minds of the company and thus with the directors,... This control can be delegated to officers whose power consists of the ability to make management and policy decisions and carry responsibility for them although the delegating director will also retain equal (joint and several) liability. (Lockett, 1996, p. 240)

This simple description of director liability clearly encompasses all decisions, policy and actions of an organisation in respect of environmental performance. Such liability is not a new concept; it has been an issue facing company directors for some time but only recently applied to environmental issues. It is clear that any system of organisational management must reflect a chain of authority that deals with the potential liabilities. Environmental compliance (both statutory and non-statutory) must be at the heart of this system, and, as previously noted, regulatory and policy issues are constantly changing. To minimise directors' and managers' liability an organisation should undertake management training which sets out the issues and gives solutions.

Environmental Reporting

As organisations become more involved with developing community relationships so they must address the information that they are required to or chose to disclose. Environmental reporting is a very formalised method of communicating with the various users of that information. Reporting may be a simple process of communicating the progress made in a given period or it may be a more detailed and complex process of providing information on liabilities and the extent of legal compliance.

Some reporting will be the unwanted, negative disclosure of poor environmental performance to a growing media sector devoted to uncovering such activities. ENDS has a reputation as the leading magazine reporting on environmental performance much of which is publicly available information on court cases. This reporting is uncontrolled and requires reactive action to be taken. An organisation which takes action to promote its performance in a controlled manner clearly takes the associated benefits.

The 1997 KPMG survey looked at environmental reporting in the major public companies in the UK (the FTSE 100). Results show that about 80% reported in 1997 on environmental matters. Thirty per cent produced a separate report dealing with environmental issues and about half that figure showed quantifiable targets.

Benefits of Environmental Reporting

The business benefits have been observed to include:

*   stronger internal commitment to improved environmental performance (note that it is the past tense and not 'improving' – which tends to reflect what might be described as a rather congratulatory role in these respects);

*   the ability to demonstrate progress in environmental management to stakeholders;

*   identifying areas where management systems need to be strengthened;

*   better PR and increased employee awareness of the environmental policies and goals of the company.

In general, the benefits are intangible but remain desirable. In public companies there is a clear peer pressure being exerted to undertake and continue the reporting of environmental performance. This, in itself, cannot be justified for reporting is expensive – usually in terms of internal resources – and if undertaken in a half-hearted way is probably not cost effective.

Legal Requirements for Reporting

In some countries legislation exists requiring environmental reporting in some form or other. For example:

- **USA:** the Securities and Exchange Commission require disclosure of the capital expenditure which arises as a result of the various legal systems at state and federal levels;

- **Canada:** has similar requirements to the USA for public companies;

- **Denmark:** from fiscal year 1996 approximately 3,000 companies must prepare 'Green Accounts'.

The focus of these statutory reports varies from place to place. In the US and Canada focus is placed on financial reporting, whereas Danish and Dutch requirements are focused on reporting environmental performance.

In the UK corporate reporting is voluntary. It is important to remember that many companies regulated under Part I of the Environmental Protection Act 1990, Water Resources Act 1991, Water Industries Act 1991 and the Waste Management Licensing Regulations are required to submit information onto a public register. Also any organisation which is required to undertake an Environmental Assessment prior to a major development project must make this information available to the public for inspection as part of the planning consultation process. This information may then be viewed by all with an interest in environmental performance. Information held on a public register is generally not financial in nature but covers environmental performance, such as discharge consent levels, authorised emission limits or the issuing of notices, and most importantly monitoring data relating to the site and its activities. Companies with information in the public domain should audit the contents of the register that applies to them – it is my experience that sometimes regulators are perhaps not as careful in controlling the contents as they should be.

Many organisations are now choosing to take control of the nature and extent of the environmental information they release into the public arena by producing their own corporate report. How a company reports, as part of the main annual report or as a separate document, should depend upon the requirements of the intended audience. If stakeholders, in addition to shareholders, are the intended audience then it is apparent that a separate report will create value particularly in terms of accountability. If the report is to focus on concerns expressed by a local community then a site-specific report may be necessary.

External Verification

External verification is growing slowly. By obtaining independent external verification a company can help to reassure its audience of the accuracy of the report's contents. Companies which have reports verified support the process, but they remain a minority, presumably because others do not see that the additional cost provides added benefit. It is perhaps this factor which has led to UK companies favouring the non-reporting standard ISO14001 over EMAS which requires an environmental statement.

The lack of any comprehensively accepted verification criteria has put off many companies. The reader of an environmental report will be aware of the differences in the statement of verification. The difference in the expert's statement varies according to the professional status of the verifiers; compare statements by audit companies, accountants and environmental consultants.

There no ground rules for verifiers – but it may be useful to demonstrate the process that I have adopted in verification (which I do not advocate to be the best way). The closest analogy of the approach I can give is the examination of a thesis – another form of long written document. An environmental report contains, essentially, two different components: factual statements and opinion. Any factual statement must be verified as accurate, which may mean that the verifier traces the origin of data and tracks through all the stages of transfer and alteration through to its entry in the report. For example, a common feature of reports is the inclusion of indicators (KPI or sustainability) which represent a number derived from primary data and converted to an environmentally relevant figure (e.g. diesel consumption represented as CO_2 and NO_X emissions). The whole process needs to be scrutinised to satisfy the verifier (and therefore the reader) that the number presented in the report is accurate. Statements of opinion need to be treated slightly differently – and to a degree the verifier should either ignore them or assess whether the opinion is based either on accepted opinion or can be justified by data presented elsewhere.

Assessment of Appropriate Reporting Methodology

An organisation should consider, in a logical manner, whether to go beyond its legal obligation, and report on environmental performance. Table 3.2 contains a process of question and answer which could help an organisation to determine if it should report.

Table 3.2 Ask Yourself If and How You Should Report

1)	Are your competitors reporting on environmental performance? If no, can you identify a business benefit if you take the lead in your sector?
2)	Does your environmental performance stand up to the rigours of reporting?
3)	Do you have the resources to dedicate to environmental communications?
4)	Will an environmental report contain quantified information on performance?
5)	Do you have sufficient data of appropriate accuracy to include in the report?
6)	Are any stakeholders requesting information on environmental performance?

If the answer to these six simple questions point towards producing an environmental report you should then ask the questions in Table 3.3 to determine in detail what process should be adopted.

The rationale behind each set of questions and the options for action should be obvious. It is clear that the perceived requirements of the stakeholders are very important in determining how to report and whether or not to verify. But overshadowing these considerations is cost – clearly separate, verified site-specific reports will be more expensive than a few paragraphs and a copy of the environmental policy statement in the corporate annual report.

One way of determining how environmental reporting should be structured and delivered is to ask the various stakeholders what information they need. Some companies do this by asking recipients of their reports to provide feedback. This process could be seen as a simple public relations exercise unless a response is made to all the feedback – however impracticable or outlandish the suggested improvement might be.

Table 3.3 Determining the Nature of the Report

Question	Answer	Action
Do all or most stakeholders require or request environmental performance information?	Yes	Separate report
	No	Combined report
OR		
Can reporting enhance internal commitment?		
Are stakeholders likely to be suspicious of the report's findings?	Yes	Verify
OR	No	No need to verify
Has environmental performance improvement stagnated?		
Is the company engaged in local community activities and actions?	Yes	Separate site reports
	No	Corporate report

Selling the Message

The method by which information is presented in reports must be managed carefully. This does not mean that information should be excluded or 'massaged' in any way. Some information will need to be explained so that confusion can be avoided. In some cases, when a process is changed, it will result in what appears to be increased negative impact when, in fact, behind this headline is a positive impact, either directly or indirectly. For example, a new process may produce a greater volume of waste but of a lower toxicity in comparison to the previous process it has replaced, so data should be presented in support of this direct benefit. An indirect benefit may be the change to less polluting or renewable raw material. Without the right technical explanation these two may be misunderstood – and the local newspaper carries a story with the headline 'Local firm creates more waste' – when the correct headline should have read 'Local firm reduces pollution'. This type of data analysis and technical interpretation may require outside expertise to produce an appropriate message which is based on sound scientific principles.

Environmental Indicators

Indicators form the basis of the message, and can be produced using an objective assessment of the impact. This requires a reasonably high level of sophistication, going beyond an assessment based simply on the weight of materials emitted without any regard for the relative or absolute hazard of those materials. An excellent example of this particular issue is the difference between different 'greenhouse gases' in terms of their global warming potential (GWP). GWP takes account of the differences in the capability of various gases to enhance the greenhouse effect (*see* Table 3.4). Local issues often present more complicated and costly problems for an individual company. But little relevant and accurate information exists for the peculiar local environmental issues because a significant proportion of the world's scientific community is working on climate change and publishing GWP indices whereas in comparison few are working on local issues.

Table 3.4 Some Examples of Global Warming Potentials, Referenced to Absolute GWP for Carbon Dioxide

Substance	Formula	Lifetime (yr)	Global warming potential	
			20 years	*100 years*
Methane	CH_4	14.5 ± 2.5	62	24.5
CFC-11	$CFCl_3$	50 ± 5	5000	4000
Carbon tetrachloride	CCl_4	42	2000	1400
Sulphur hexafluoride	SF_6	3200	16500	24900

A simple, but not entirely convincing, way around this is to use normalised data. This form of data presents information as a form of environmental efficiency. The approach cannot hope to address the relative environmental impact of two substances, but merely provides an indication of the process efficiency. Normalisation is not worse, just different, and this must be recognised when communicating performance information to the public.

Normalisation can be a real benefit for organisations which are growing or setting targets within an environmental management system. Compare the two sets of statements from imaginary environmental reports in Table 3.5.

Table 3.5 Raw and Normalised Data

	Raw data	Normalised data
1996	300 tonnes of controlled waste	2 tonnes of waste per thousand tonnes of product
1997	450 tonnes of controlled waste	1.5 tonnes of waste per thousand tonnes of product

In 1996 300 tonnes of waste were produced from 150,000 tonnes of product, but in 1997 production increased to 300,000 tonnes. The raw waste data show performance has worsened (even if production tonnage is included in another part of the report it will not be associated with the waste unless explicitly linked), but in terms of production efficiency performance has improved. This is an important message, as without improved efficiency the 1997 raw data would have been 600 tonnes or 33% worse.

There is a selection of possible factors that can be used to indicate efficiency. The normalising factor must be relevant to the basic data that it is used in conjunction with. There is no right answer, but some combinations work better than others, while some combinations can actually be misleading. Table 3.6 shows some possible combinations.

Alternative Methods of Communicating Your Message

Alternative methods to formal reports exist for communicating a targeted message of interest to specific stakeholders. These are as varied as the particular stakeholders' requirements and the nature of the information to be delivered.

Many companies now communicate through statements on products. This has long been established in the paper industry where the recycled paper content of a product has been provided to customers. This type of message has long been a concern of the consumer protection organisations and may be subject to accusations of being misleading. Some companies have now recognised this – it was recently reported, for example, that Sainsbury plc would be reviewing the claims of environmental performance of its own brands. This form of communications audit is time consuming and expensive, but will help to strengthen the veracity of the message and any claims being made.

Table 3.6　Environmental Indicator Matrix

Basic data	Product output	Material inputs	Energy input	Water input	Employees	Workdays	Working hours	Building space	Sales	Production costs
Materials input	✔									
Packaging	✔	✔								
Cleaning agents								✔		
Energy input	✔				✔		✔	✔		
Water input	✔				✔					
Waste	✔	✔								
Waste water	✔			✔						
Air emissions	✔		✔							
Transportation	✔				✔					
Workplace accidents					✔	✔	✔			
Complaints/prosecutions						✔				
Training					✔	✔				
Environmental costs									✔	✔

Some companies use catalogues to communicate their commitment to environmental issues. In the past this might have painted a glowing picture, but increasing awareness and cynicism amongst consumers has meant that the alert business will promote a more realistic message. An excellent example of this is Ikea – the Swedish furniture and household goods chain of shops. In one of their recent catalogues there is a double page devoted to their environmental philosophy.

At IKEA we don't want to fool ourselves – and we certainly don't want to fool you.

We know that, if our products are to be environmentally compatible, we must be strict and set ourselves very high standards.

To us, adapting our range to the environment means manufacturing products so that the materials, techniques and transport we use have as little impact as possible on the natural environment. That means making the most rational use of raw materials and never letting anything go to waste.

This is why we are honest enough to say that, so far, only three of our products are genuinely adapted to the environment.

Next year our environmentally adapted range will be much, much larger.

Already we have hundreds of products which meet almost all of the high standards we have imposed. But for us, nearly is not quite enough.

To be environmentally compatible, a product must meet every single one. Plenty of people claim that their products are environmentally friendly. But ask yourself. Can any manufacturing process actually be good for the environment? Perhaps a more honest approach is to think ecologically. That's what we do at IKEA.

We do our best not to consume resources at a rate faster than Nature can replace them. That's why you won't find any wood from tropical rainforests at IKEA.

We strive to use only materials and substances which can be broken down naturally.

And we are determined to minimise waste. That's why we've introduced pilot schemes for recycling products, packaging and paper.

Our long-term aim is to proceed with a series of small, well planned steps towards a truly more sustainable society.

It's not enough just being friendly to the environment. We must adapt to it. We, you and everyone else must adapt ourselves to the forests, the seas, the fresh air and the mountains.

It's we who must change — not them.

Let us look in more detail at this statement compared to previous statements of environmental friendliness from the 1980s and early 1990s.

- It addresses what the company does and how it interacts with the environment and its customers.

- It makes open statements implying imperfection, but promises real improvements.

- It addresses long-term improvement, not short-term platitudes.

In an increasingly sophisticated consumer marketplace this type of message must, however, be substantiated. There are many individuals and organisations which will knock such an apparently honest statement of intent. Indeed there are many holes in such a statement, but the current trends show this form is becoming more common.

Environmentally Sound Investments

Earlier in this chapter I looked at the liabilities to which lenders may be exposed to and how they are responding – or not – to environmental risks. One area where concern is being realised in the decision-making process is in ethical investment.

It has become increasingly apparent that we want our investments to be with companies that do not harm the environment or human health. There has been a growth in fund market products which deliver on this issue. The ethical investment sector is still small in comparison to conventional schemes, but it is growing and the products appear to perform well. Investors have been conservative in their approach to environmental performance and this is seen as a weakness in some heavy industry sectors where improvements have been made over the past years.

In the short term a business which invests heavily in new technologies of pollution prevention ahead of its competitors may appear to be less attractive to an investor. But in an ever changing regulatory and policy environment this active, innovative company will benefit from being ahead of the competition. Investors interested in a long-term strategy will be attracted to this company even though its short-term performance is affected by this capital investment.

A Friends Provident/NOP Ethical Investment survey in 1997 showed that 94% of British adults agreed with the statement – 'I want my investment to benefit companies which are helping rather than harming the world.' So there exists a demand for ethical investment products. How do investors develop a portfolio of clients which do indeed help rather than harm the world? An example of a common approach is provided by Friends Provident – what they call 'The Stewardship Investment

Approach'. Investments are assessed by an independent panel of experts on a case-by-case basis using both positive and negative criteria (*see* Table 3.7). It is clear that value judgements have been made in the case of some of the criteria. The way in which these criteria are applied is not entirely clear in the publications of these fund management companies and there is a need for greater accountability in the use of criteria such as these. As investors become more informed of the choices available to them, so the investment funds making such claims of environmental and ethical standards need to review their procedures and selection criteria.

Table 3.7 Criteria for Assessing Investments – Friends Provident Stewardship Approach

Positive criteria	Negative criteria
Supplying the basic necessities of life	Environmental damage and pollution
Providing high quality products and services	Unnecessary exploitation of animals
which are of long-term benefit to the	Trade or operations in oppressive regimes
community	Exploitation of Third World countries
Conservation of energy and natural resources	Manufacture and sale of weapons
Good relations with customers and suppliers	Nuclear power, including construction of plant and
Good employment practices	equipment and supply, transport and disposal of
Training and education	nuclear materials
Strong community involvement	Tobacco or alcohol production (more than 10% of
A good equal opportunities record	production activity)
Openness about company activities	Gambling, pornography and offensive or misleading
	advertising

It is worth mentioning that companies like Friends Provident also offer investment funds which do not require assessment against these criteria. Those with an interest in ethical funds openly state that they will set out to influence those not taking the benefits of stewardship type funds. Ethical investment funds can exert some pressure on corporate performance but it is very early days in the UK and pressure will be dictated by the performance of these funds (*see* Table 3.8). What is apparent is that companies which can take advantage now of these investment funds will be able to claim commercial advantage and the improved profile of being in the vanguard.

Table 3.8 Performance of Investment Funds in the Last Five Years
(Reported in the *Guardian*, 17th January 1998)

Fund	£1,000 after 5 years	% growth
Credit Suisse Fellowship	£2,083.93	108.4
Framlington Health	£2,000.00	100.0
TSB Environmental Investor	£1,894.78	89.5
Friends Provident Stewardship	£1,816.79	81.7
Sovereign Ethical	£1,812.16	81.2
United Charities	£1,793.50	79.4
Scottish Equitable Ethical	£1,762.30	76.2
NPI Global Care	£1,728.79	72.9
Jupiter Ecology	£1,727.71	72.8
Friends Provident Stewardship N. America	£1,715.99	71.6
CIS Environ	£1,694.09	69.4
City Financial Acron Ethical	£1,660.11	66.0
Allchurches Amity	£1,650.25	65.0
Friends Provident Stewardship Inc	£1,642.29	64.2
Sector Average	**£1,732.48**	**73.3**

That the funds generally perform well reinforces the cliché that good environmental (ethical) management equals good business management. Cynicism exists because the criteria remain relatively subjective. This will remain so unless expensive research is undertaken against performance norms or targets against each application to join a fund manager's list.

The results suggest that the funds perform well for all concerned – for the investor, the corporate body and the fund manager. While the market remains small, the individual investor wishing to invest with those who do not harm the environment (relatively) can be reasonably certain that the criteria are used properly to assess companies in which investment is placed. But as the market grows and becomes more competitive, it could be argued that these standards might be lowered, making the confidence of the investor less certain. Therefore it remains the duty of the funds and its managers to ensure that appropriate standards are met and accountability is maintained. After all, questions about a fund will only be asked if it does not perform well compared to others – good performance does not deserve similar scrutiny.

Benchmarking

Benchmarking has long been recognised as beneficial to business. It provides an objective method of assessing the relative performance of companies in similar sectors. It is a way of assessing performance against your competitors or between divisions within the same company. It has led to the principle of the 'world class performer'. Benchmarking environmental performance is embryonic. It remains the case that few established and recognised figures exist against which an organisation may assess itself.

Internally Set Benchmarks

The simplest form of internal benchmark is the legal limit placed on a substance in official permits, authorisations and consents.

An organisation may set up its own internal benchmarks but this can only lead to a degree of stagnation (*see also* Table 3.6). Let's take an example to illustrate the point. If a company wishes to benchmark its company car fuel economy performance then it would probably take the best fuel economy figures of each make and model used and compare this against each individual driver's fuel consumption figures. A league table might then be established – perhaps ranking performance as the ratio of individual consumption against manufacturers' specification. Thus if your average consumption is 35 mpg against the manufacturers' specification of 70 mpg you score 50% and rank below me because my ratio is 55 mpg against 70 mpg or about 79%. All this achieves is interpersonal competition, not inter-company competition against established benchmarks. Further, in this particular example there is an incentive to move to cars with poorer fuel economy because it is easier to achieve a higher percentage score when working against a lower manufacturers' specification. It is not satisfactory.

Externally Set Benchmarks

Publicly available data do exist for energy consumption in buildings of different types. These simple normalised values can be quickly compared against the performance of any company's buildings and the activities undertaken. These data have been developed and are updated by the Buildings Research Establishment and Energy Efficiency Best Practice Programme in line with the introduction of new buildings and facilities management techniques. A variety of buildings and activities are covered and an indication of the cost of heating, lighting and powering equipment is provided. The process of producing the initial data on specific consumption is relatively simple and guidance is provided by the Energy Efficiency Best Practice Programme. The benchmark provides a single value against which performance can be assessed (or audited). The focus of this particular exercise is to reduce the costs incurred by organisations of running buildings and infrastructure – so the benefit is clearly cost savings. It has been estimated that using this simple technique most companies have the potential to save up to 20% on their energy spend for little or no capital expenditure.

Benchmarking will become more common and easier to undertake, but also more rigorous as reporting of environmental performance grows in popularity. An environmental manager can then quickly assess performance against a competitor. For example, the water companies are able to benchmark leakage of mains water both against each other and against the requirements of the regulator. All of this information is in the public domain, which can provide additional motivation to improve.

Responding to Stakeholder Requirements

IBM has undertaken research into the parameters which stakeholders wish to see reported. The results of the research show a number of areas commonly used in environmental reports but also identify a number of less familiar parameters. Table 3.9 reproduces the interpretation of the research.

Table 3.9 Stakeholder Ranking – IBM Survey (1996)

Parameter	Priority ranking
Environmental management	Very high priority
IT/sustainable development	Very high priority
Products	Very high priority
Customers	Very high priority
Suppliers	High priority
Energy	High priority
Global	High priority
Transport	High priority
Commercial	Priority
Manufacturing	Priority
Culture	Priority

These data were then used to benchmark existing performance against while taking into account the relative priority given to each parameter by stakeholders. In this way IBM could give attention to the areas of most importance to the stakeholder.

Benchmarking Corporate Performance

In the past two years an attempt has been made to produce an assessment of corporate environmental engagement by the FTSE 100 companies, undertaken by Business in the Environment. The index for each company responding to the survey was calculated from scores given to levels of engagement in ten sections. These sections were: Corporate Environmental Policy, Board-Level Commitment, Environmental Management System, Published Environmental Objectives, Measurable Targets, Internal Environmental Audit Programme, Environmental Stewardship, Environment-Focused Supplier Programme and Regular Environmental Communication with Stakeholders. The overall score, expressed as a percentage of complete engagement, was then placed into statistical quintiles to enable comparison. So the best performing (most engaged) companies were in the first and worst performing in the fifth quintiles. The benchmarking was relative. The absolute scores are irrelevant because each year the boundary scores for each quintile will change, increasing as performance is improved. This is borne out by the quintile scores in 1996 and 1997 (Table 3.10). For example, a score of 50% in 1996 would have the company in the 4th quintile, but the same score in 1997 would result in a 5th quintile placing. This exercise encourages, through a form of peer group pressure, companies to improve.

Table 3.10 Improved Performance of the FTSE 100
(From 'The Index of Corporate Environmental Engagement – 1996 and 1997')

	1996	1997
1st quintile	83 – 94%	86.4 – 98%
2nd quintile	69 – 81%	73.2 – 86%
3rd quintile	57 – 68%	66.8 – 72.9%
4th quintile	47 – 56%	52.3 – 63.1%
5th quintile	3 – 42%	0 – 51.8%

The intention of such an exercise is two-fold:

•   It allows direct comparison between companies which have very different environmental aspects and impact, for example HSBC plc and BP, and thus allows very different companies the opportunity to benchmark their environmental performance.

•   It provides a campaigning tool to promote environmental engagement in the country's leading public companies.

Whichever way the results are used the effect on businesses is that they need to gain a better understanding of their environmental engagement. Going through the process can also be advantageous to other companies (outside the FTSE 100 or privately or foreign owned) because it focuses the mind of senior management on the strengths and weaknesses of the organisation they lead in terms of environmental performance.

Economic Instruments or Green Taxation

In the recently published book *Factor Four* (*see* Further reading) it is suggested that we need to turn our attention to rewarding behaviour which promotes sustainable activities as opposed to the present situation where we are supporting behaviour which is unsustainable. Green taxes are a way of penalising activities considered to be against the principles of sustainability. Green taxes are not particularly new, nor as they stand at the moment are they significantly different from some forms of existing regulation of the environment. What needs to be appreciated is that they have been made a stated objective of the EU Fifth Environment Action Programme and UK government policy.

Green Taxes

If we define a tax as being 'a contribution exacted by the state' then one might consider that any licence fee payable to an environment agency is a form of green tax. In practice though, a green tax is more tightly defined either as a fiscal measure or instrument, which make markets work for the environment or as 'taxes and charges … to cover all compulsory, unrequited payments, whether the revenue accrues directly to the Government budget or is destined for particular purposes'. However, the complexity of the market makes such instruments difficult to develop. Indeed while industry remains distrustful of such innovative approaches to environmental protection, the scope for voluntary industry sector or product agreements seems remote especially when we also consider the complexity involved in developing effective economic instruments.

There are largely two forms of green taxation: taxes on emissions and taxes on products (e.g. IPC authorisation fees and landfill tax respectively). Both forms would seek to achieve the principles of sustainable development. We have long used fees to reflect the burden of polluting emissions through discharge, trade effluent consents and IPC and APC authorisations. These fees are often considered as being a part of the 'command and control' approach to environmental regulation and it is here that the distinction between the two methods becomes blurred. At present we have a number of fiscal measures aimed at products designed and implemented as green taxes:

- fuel price differentiation;

- VAT on domestic fuel;

- the landfill tax; and

- most recently, the Producer Responsibility Obligations (Packaging Waste) Regulations 1997.

The use of the revenue, or earmarking, is an associated feature of green taxes as economic instruments. It has been argued that in order to facilitate improvements in environmental quality the revenue from green taxes should be targeted at suitable issues and earmarked accordingly. This approach can lead to fiscal inefficiency, so that the revenue will dictate the amount available rather than the amount available reflecting the real need. In other words, if revenue from a green tax is directed towards reducing national insurance contributions (as is the case with the landfill tax), then as waste reduces so does the revenue. At the same time there is a need to maintain that level of funding of NI which is not directly related to this revenue source, so funds need to be sought from elsewhere. This can lead to an abuse of the underlying purpose because the temptation exists to raise the rate of the taxation to offset the fall in revenue.

Recent Approaches to Green Taxation

Although past UK administrations have advocated deregulation, it seems to have missed the opportunity to achieve this, at least in part, through economic instruments. It did introduce or enhance the forms of taxation referred to above and the new government undoubtedly has a greater resolve in addressing and championing environmental issues.

- Fuel price differentiation was used initially in conjunction with other legal instruments so that new petrol driven motor cars were required to run on unleaded fuel. Due to the fact that many cars can be adjusted to take unleaded fuel, a price differentiation has remained and has been constantly increased between leaded and unleaded petrol. This is a very obvious use of pricing policy to affect our behaviour to the benefit of the environment, at least in terms of the lead emitted by motor vehicles.

- VAT on domestic fuel was introduced to raise revenue for the Exchequer. The rationale behind it was not initially seen as a green tax, but in effect it acts as one by increasing the price and increasing awareness. The revenue from these first two taxes is not used to fund environmental projects but as a general method of raising tax revenue.

- The landfill tax was introduced in the Finance Act 1996 and is regulated through the Landfill Tax Regulations 1996; it is aimed at taxing waste at the point of disposal in order to reduce the amount of our waste going to landfill. This was in accordance with the waste strategy of encouraging re-use and recycling of waste materials. The landfill tax has been estimated by HM Customs and Excise to have generated in its first year some £450 million in revenue, of which 20% or some £90 million can be directed towards environmental bodies which can then use it to perform environmental good works according to the relevant conditions. This green tax exhibits many of the principles described above. It aims to change behaviour by increasing the cost to society of waste disposal to landfill through the use of an economic instrument rather than a command and control form of regulation. Further, it uses a part of the tax revenue to remediate and fund environmental projects to the general benefit of society.

- The packaging levy which has been imposed by the introduction of the Producer Responsibility Obligations (Packaging Waste) Regulations 1997 is yet to come into full force. Although the regulations do not appear to make reference to green taxes, the purchase of Packaging Reprocessing Notes (PRNs) is in effect a fiscal instrument designed to encourage producers and sellers to review the use and types of packaging with a view to reducing the overall quantity in circulation and being disposed of in landfill sites. It is too early to assess or even describe how this will operate in practice, but many industry bodies have described it as a tax on packaging. One of the stated aims of the regulations is to increase the capacity in the UK to recover and recycle packaging waste, so like the landfill tax it will be using some of the revenue to achieve the aims of sustainability.

Other New Initiatives

There are many new schemes being suggested. Traditional approaches to regulation of the environment are being increasingly challenged by pressure and interest groups and in response alternatives are being considered or put into action. The accusation is that the traditional process is not delivering the intended environmental improvements (*see* Further reading). In order to address this concern in the UK, we are looking elsewhere in the world for ideas from which initiatives may be developed in the UK. All new ideas are then put through an extensive process of public and expert consultation to determine the relevance and applicability of the particular innovation. A business seeking to comply should keep up to date with the debate and attempt to assess the relevance to its own activities or product, in exactly the same way as they would with new legislation. Below I review two such initiatives, covenants and tradable permits. Both are systems of compliance used elsewhere in the world and are being considered, to a greater or lesser extent, in the UK. These initiatives are difficult to classify as either statutory or non-statutory – I have chosen to place it in the latter category because the processes under consideration are, like green taxes, not a traditional normative style of regulation.

Covenants

Producer responsibility has already been addressed in Chapter 2, but other versions of this approach exist. In the Netherlands successful covenants have been negotiated between industry and government. Under these covenants the two parties agree to set and monitor against targets to improve performance in the selected activity. The covenants exist outside the traditional normative approach favoured in the UK. Formal covenants do not find favour in the UK, I believe, because there is a degree of mistrust between industry and government. The approach does offer a practical solution to the problems perceived to exist with the traditional approach.

Tradable Permits

In USA, there is a system of permits which allows a polluter to trade in a market their allowance for certain substances. At the moment the system is used for emissions to air of greenhouse gases.

Without going into excessive detail, the system allows those that wish to increase their emissions of pollutants to do so if they can find someone who has an excess capacity for that pollutant. If a company currently emits 1,000 megatonnes of carbon dioxide, but wants to increase to 2,000 megatonnes then it must pay on an open market for the extra capacity. Conversely, if a company introduces pollution prevention measures that cause a reduction in emissions, then they may wish to sell into the market their new excessive permits, thus providing a positive revenue from pollution prevention. There is a finite quantity of units or permits available within a specified geographical area so there is an upper limit.

In the UK consultation is currently underway to explore the possibilities of adapting or adopting a similar process for discharges into rivers and estuaries. A river or reach of a river or estuary has a carrying capacity for a given pollutant, referred to as an environmental quality standard (EQS). The challenge presented by this initiative is the complex make-up of discharges into a river. The combination of households discharging through sewers to water treatment facilities and industrial process, transportation system (road drains) and agricultural pollutants makes for an interesting cocktail, but most importantly an extremely diverse set of organisations. In practice trading permits is only feasible for large, individual polluters using a single, identifiable point to discharge the polluting matter. Scale is important in this issue. In a similar way, large institutional shareholders possess greater power than the combined power of private shareholders in a public company, so a large discharger has a greater ability to control a market in tradable pollutants permits.

It will be interesting to see what results. I remain unconvinced that such an approach will improve the situation and achieve the desired goal of better quality river water. What is obvious, though, is that the compliance options will increase and become more complex. A company wishing to stay abreast of the situation should begin to study these initiatives in the same way that they track the progression of policy into new legislation.

Developing a Strategy for Improvement

If an organisation wishes to gain a benefit by addressing these various economic instruments and new initiatives, then it must set out a strong internal strategy. These measures do not rely on an environmental regulator for enforcement. The landfill tax is regulated by HM Customs and Excise, which only has a duty to ensure that the tax revenue is collected. They do not have any incentive to see the level of tax revenue fall due to better environmental performance – in this case the quantity of waste being disposed of to registered landfill. A business must, therefore, set out its own 'regulatory' regime to ensure that the commercial benefits can be realised through better waste management practices.

The simplest regime is effective auditing of such practices (*see* Chapter 4). An internal strategy must set objectives which can be reviewed at regular intervals and these objectives should include non-statutory compliance issues. One of the easiest ways of keeping an eye on progress is to use the Internet. All the government departments and Environment Agency have excellent and informative websites which are regularly updated and interactive.

Summary

Non-statutory environmental compliance requires a slightly different approach to that adopted for compliance with regulations. Underlying this approach, however, remains the need to understand the interaction of a great range of external influences on the activities and products of the company. It cannot be overstated that any organisation, seeking to realise the benefits from the pressures being exerted from these wide range of sources outside traditional regulatory agencies, must be fully aware of the risks, requirement criteria and liabilities.

Non-statutory compliance issues have emerged in the past five to ten years and continue to develop. Their existence needs to be recognised and acted on – for it is unlikely to diminish. Unlike statutory issues – where action to comply should be a given condition of business activity – these issues need to be identified and prioritised to ensure that the most benefit can be assured without excessive draining of resources. Most of the benefits remain intangible, but a business seeking to take a competitive advantage should be addressing such issues in a way which goes beyond conventional economic analyses.

CHAPTER 4

Environmental Management Systems: Compliance Issues

Introduction

Environmental management systems (EMS) have emerged as the management tool of the 1990s. With the launch of both BS7750/ISO14001 and eco-management and audit schemes (EMAS), we have seen the formal recognition of environmental management in mainstream business activities. The number of companies developing EMS is still relatively small; however, as more become certificated and verified (depending on the particular system) so more will see the benefits or be 'encouraged' to start.

Companies are developing EMS for a variety of reasons – some of which will have been discussed elsewhere – therefore this report will not repeat the benefits and opportunities that arise from EMS. For the same reason I shall not detail what an EMS is – but shall simply provide two well established definitions (to ensure we are all talking about the same thing).

ISO14001: 1996

> *that part of the overall management system which includes organisational structure, planning activities, responsibilities, practices, procedures, processes and resources for developing, implementing, acheiving, reviewing and maintaining the environmental policy.*

Eco-management and audit scheme (EMAS)

that part of the overall management system which includes the organisational structure, responsibilities, practices, procedures, processes and resources for determining and implementing the environmental policy.

The main emphasis being placed on EMS is that it is a method to improve operational efficiency through cost-saving projects that can be broadly described as waste minimisation or energy efficiency. In the longer term, however, EMS allows firms to assess, manage and develop strategically taking into account the environmental impacts of their activities. In this particular aspect EMS is potentially going to be either an opportunity or a threat. An organisation which does not take the legal implications and responsibilities seriously will or may find itself in difficulty. Those that have considered the law appropriately during the development and implementation of the EMS will be in a strong commercial position (providing the system operates properly over the coming years). Those which are looking to EMS as a cheap, quick public relations fix may be placing themselves in a risky situation.

This chapter will explore some of the legal implications of environmental management systems. Particular attention will be given to the policy statement, organisation and personnel responsibility, and the environmental aspects and impacts register, with additional comment on the legal implications of audit and reporting.

Environmental Management Systems in the Regulatory Context

The existence of a legal framework is the major difference between quality and environmental management systems. While the quality system allows you to manage your operations and product in terms of the customer, the EMS assists in the management of your legal obligations and liabilities and in your relationship with the environmental regulators as well as with other stakeholders.

The development and implementation of an EMS cannot of itself provide a company with assurance that its performance not only meets, but will continue to meet, legislative and policy requirements.

There are, however, two basic principles whichever system or system standard an organisation chooses:

• the EMS is built around relevant legal requirements; and

- the EMS operates in such a way as to be functional at all scales in the organisation and for every eventuality.

A thorough review of the legal requirements allows the EMS to exist in a framework of external controls. Unlike the ISO9000 series an organisation cannot escape the external control of environmental regulators and legislation. Mere compliance with internally established and auditable limits or standards is only part of the EMS. If an EMS allows an organisation to confuse system non-conformance and legal non-compliance then it places that organisation in a potentially serious situation.

Environmental Management Systems as a Part of Existing Legislation

It should not be forgotten that any business operating a prescribed process under Part 1 (Integrated Pollution Control (IPC)) of the Environmental Protection Act 1990 has already developed a quasi-EMS through the application and authorisation process. In the Chief Inspector's Guidance to Inspectors Process Guidance Notes IPR series there is the outline of an EMS for the purposes of complying with the Part. Most of the aspects are present: a systematic approach to monitoring and reporting, an overall policy objective, targets etc. (*see* Table 4.1). In addition to the IPC application and authorisation process there is now information on risk assessment from the Environment Agency.

The principle of continuous improvement (particularly in formal system standards such as ISO14001 and EMAS) is also explicit in Environmental Protection Act 1990 Part I procedures and legislation. BATNEEC is an evolving concept. As technology advances so the 'best available technique' changes. Companies are required to comply with BATNEEC in the upgrading programme established by the appropriate pollution regulator.

So, since 1990, companies that are operating prescribed processes have had a form of EMS. This has allowed them to comply with the requirements of BATNEEC and establish a working relationship with the appropriate regulator. A comprehensive, fully functional EMS will, however, offer more than mere management of pollution regulation compliance.

Table 4.1 A Comparison of Key EMS Stages with Guidance for IPC Compliance Using a Set of the Environment Agency Guidance Notes

EMS Stage	IPR 4/11	
Environmental Policy	2.1.1	'Processes ... must be operated with the objective of ensuring that ... the best available technique not entailing excessive cost (BATNEEC) will be used' for preventing the release, or for rendering harmless or for minimising the pollution which may be caused to the environment.
Environmental Review/ Register of Environmental Aspects and Impacts	2.2 2.2.2 2.4	Application and authorisations documentation especially (a) provide full information on the selection of the primary process, particularly for a new process; and (b) provide evidence that the requirement to use BATNEEC will be met. Process assessment and release minimisation programme Plus: Annex 1 'Processes'
Targets and Objectives	3.2.3	'All existing processes should be upgraded with the aim of achieving the standards ... for new plant at the earliest opportunity and generally no later than 1 November 1997.'
Programme	3.2.4	A programme indicating areas of the process requiring upgrading and the techniques to be used should be included in the application. 'A detailed programme should be submitted within 6 months of the date of issue of an authorisation and should take into account the provisions of the authorisation.'
Documentation and Control		E.g. Annex 4 1.7 'The Inspector should specify the procedures to be followed in the event of non-compliance with the condition of an authorisation.' Annex 3.13 Record keeping
Organisation and Personnel		Annex 5 Additional requirements: 1.0 Introduction 'Requirements include not only the provision of the most suitable techniques and technology, but the proper maintenance of equipment, its supervision when in use and the training and supervision of properly qualified staff.'
Reporting (EMAS only)		Annex A4 3.14

An active company may wish to move ahead of the existing limits and standards as laid down by the statutes and directives. The purpose of such an approach may be two-fold:

- to anticipate future policy trends and provide contingency funding;

- to plan for expansion (it must be remembered that most prescribed processes, effluent or abstraction consents take account of the scale of the operation – therefore planned expansion must take account of the thresholds which exist, e.g. between IPC and air pollution control (APC)).

An EMS should be used as a planning tool. The inclusion of environmental issues into the development of new ventures has been an afterthought in the past. A holistic approach will provide a strategic framework which should allow all direct and indirect aspects and impacts to be managed and minimised. This may reduce operating costs and better target capital expenditure, as well as identify legal compliance issues at an early stage.

Environmental Management Systems in Civil Proceedings

In any civil action brought against a company for negligence, the company will be judged by the courts against the standard of expertise of its peers. As a defendant, an organisation will be expected to be able to demonstrate a level of expertise and conduct equivalent to that of an 'average' company in a particular sector. As more organisations implement EMS, so the courts will view them as exemplifying good environmental practice. The courts may legitimately hold that this is the normal standard of expertise in the industry and so others will be judged accordingly. In the event of a company causing injury to someone and being sued in the civil courts for negligence, if they do not have in place an EMS they may be judged negligent as a result and be held liable for the damage or injury caused.

The courts will not necessarily know that only a small percentage of companies are operating an EMS, but they will be aware, or be made aware, of the existence of EMAS and the ISO14000 series, plus sector initiatives such as the Chemicals Industry Association's Responsible Care Management Systems for Health, Safety and Environment. A company not able to demonstrate that it operated in a manner similar to these levels of expertise would then have the burden of proof placed on them. In the case of civil law, therefore, the development of an EMS may be as a result of peer pressure, leading to acceptable norms of performance as a defence.

The Legal Implications of the Environmental Policy Statement

The policy statement is the first manifestation of the corporate approach to environmental management. Although there is no 'correct' version, there are sections or subsidiary statements which should be included. It is clear that the law provides the basis from which all policies should derive and develop and which all policies will have to take into account. Conflict between the corporate policy or guidance on implementing the policy and appropriate legislation should be avoided.

Figure 4.1 Simplified EMS Cycle

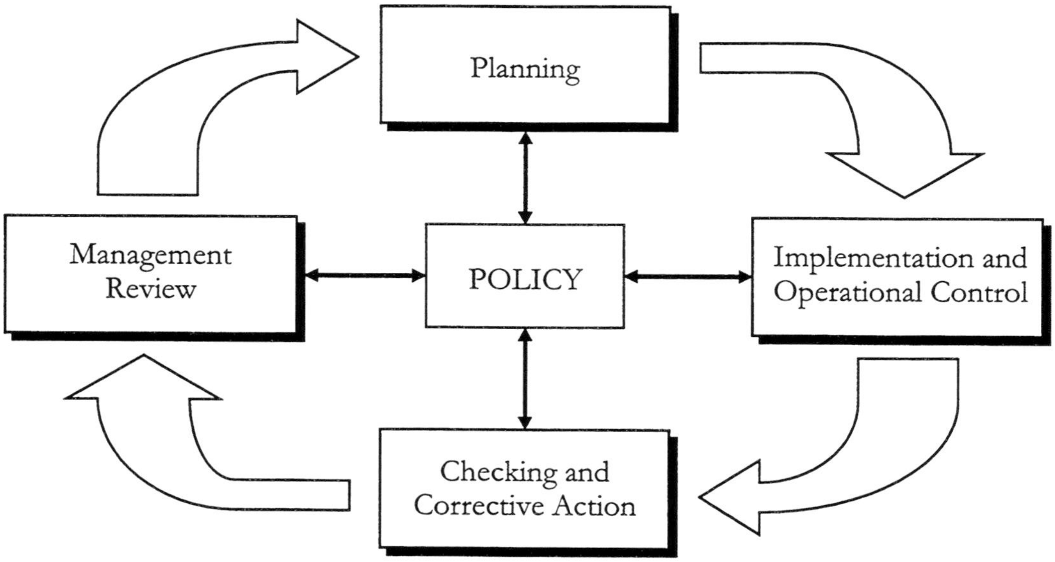

Policy Guidance

The use of guidance on the application of the policy should be seen as being good practice. Most policies contain rather vague statements of intent (see below), so should be backed up with detailed guidelines as to the specific meaning and implications of the implementation programme (see section below on internal applications). Policy guidance should be available to all in a position of authority, and certain sections may need to be more widely available. A company should consider whether it would be appropriate to consult with the relevant regulator on certain sections.

The guidance should be comprehensive and should clearly identify scales of importance, implementation and management. The guidance should be explicitly linked to other parts of the EMS (Figure 4.1), especially the policy, targets, aspects and impacts sections. Special guidance linked to other corporate policies may be separately provided for audit, monitoring and training procedures. Simply, the guidance should seek to answer the following questions:

- Why?

- When?

- Where?

- What?

- How?

From these five simple words the following should be considered for inclusion in the policy guidelines:

- Policy linkage – expand each section of the policy into an operational context.

- Applicability – in time (e.g. planning only stage) and space (e.g. sites with boilers greater than 50 MW thermal input).

- Minimum standards – corporate or legal minimum standards to be obtained to conform to the policy.

- Good practice – to achieve or go beyond minimum standards.

- Risk assessment technique – to provide consistent risk appraisal across company departments, sites or in respect of environmental aspects and impacts to different media.

The guidance should be a controlled but dynamic document. The development of the details should continue, especially as a result of initial reviews and audits. The link with the policy statement should allow for changes in European policy, for example, to be transferred to the guidance. This form of documentation is particularly useful in groups, large sites or multidisciplinary companies. It must be accompanied by training in its application and regular audits.

Internal Application of the Policy

One of the central parts of the EMS is the raising of awareness of the workforce. All staff are required to be trained in and be aware of the policy statement and if a formal standard is required, it is to be made publicly available. For example, in ISO14001 reference is made to both of the above. Many people in the 'depths' of an organisation are frequently unaware of the serious consequences of legal breaches but may be made aware through the policy statement – an opportunity not to be missed, even if no formal standard is required. In addition, if it is subsequently discovered during legal proceedings that staff were not aware of the EMS policy statement, then senior management may be considered to be doubly negligent – to have allowed a breach and not to have made all staff aware (lack of awareness of the consequences of a particular action may have been the reason for the breach in the first place).

The policy itself is not a legally binding document, with the possible exception of the potential for *misrepresentation*. Misrepresentation exists when an apparently true statement of fact induces a person to enter into a contract. Very few policies are used in this manner. The statement should not be too specific, however, it should set out the intentions of the corporate body which can be used to develop targets throughout the organisation.

For example, compare these two statements:

- 'We will reclaim all our transport packaging.'

- 'The company will seek to minimise its environmental impact from the transportation of its product.'

It is possible, if unlikely, that the first statement would leave the company open to charges of misrepresentation if it does not reclaim it from all its customers (especially the smallest), but it could result in a loss of good PR.

As the corporate programme continues so the policy should be regularly updated. Changes in the law should also provoke a reappraisal of the policy statement. While a policy is not legally binding, it is a document which indicates the organisation's stance; it is publicly available and therefore may be a plus *or* a minus in the event of legal proceedings.

The environmental policy should not be developed without due regard for the legal framework it must exist within.

Organisation and Personnel Responsibility

An EMS will provide for the allocation of responsibilities and resources. Anyone given responsibility should understand the legal obligations quite clearly. These obligations may in the worst case be criminal liabilities. The individual should, for example, be aware of the statutory provisions in S. 157 of the Environmental Protection Act 1990 which allows regulators to prosecute individuals in respect of any offence committed by the company.

In order to attract criminal liability the regulator has to show that the offence was committed by the company with the connivance or consent of, or is attributable to any neglect on any part of, an officer of the company. The result of a successful prosecution of the individual is hefty fines and possible imprisonment.

However, the courts have shown reluctance to attach criminal responsibility to those who are not in a position of authority. Therefore, an EMS must clearly define responsibility and authority – in a legal sense as well as in a management sense. This means that legal liabilities may be increased if an environmental manager does not have appropriate authority and therefore the attachment of 'guilt' may rest with the plant manager or managing director, who, in turn, may not be fully aware of the legal consequences of the effect of a change in process.

The reporting lines in the management system will allow the courts to decide the level of responsibility and therefore the consent or connivance or neglect on the part of an individual and whether that individual had the authority to control events. Companies fearing being drowned in a sea of paperwork need to be aware of its importance particularly if criminal proceedings are brought and due diligence has to be shown.

The EMS must allow for appropriate training to be available to staff including, and perhaps especially senior management. It should also ensure that records are kept. This training requirement should not be underestimated from the legal perspective. As shown above the senior management may not ignore their responsibility – their role as leaders is crucial. It is vital that document control is strictly observed and carried out by properly trained staff. Careless alteration to procedures, without due regard to the law or to the lines of authority, may result in incidents and accidents which are avoidable.

In summing up a recent case the judge made several comments that provide suitable reinforcement to these assertions.

> *It is a very long standing principle of English law that if a works causes noxious substances to be released into the air, it has to show that it used the best practicable means of preventing them being released at all or rendering them harmless if they are released. The burden is placed fairly and squarely on the business in question to educate itself about the best practicable means of achieving those aims, to set out clearly to its staff what needs to be done to achieve them, and to have an effective system of monitoring and supervision in place to identify any shortcomings by its staff.*

He went on to add:

> *In my judgement it is not only the operatives and their supervisors who are to blame for what happened. I accept that the company caused written instructions to be posted ... and that these instructions were disobeyed on the occasions I have mentioned, but I remain of the view that it is the management of the company who are most seriously to blame for not ensuring that their staff knew why they were being instructed ... and for not having effective monitoring systems in place to ensure that this did not happen, or if it did happen, it did not happen for very long. If they were using old plant, it was even more important that they should take steps to comply with their legal duties.*

Property Tenure and Environmental Management

A fundamental consideration for compliance within an environmental management system is that of property tenure – and one often left unrecognised. An organisation which has freehold of its property has obvious responsibility for its own land and therefore for the improvement or control of environmental aspects related to activities on that land. If there is a more complex arrangement of land tenure the responsibilities may become unclear.

Where land tenure is complicated it is vital for any organisation undertaking environmental management to recognise the complexities and adopt appropriate responsibilities. An organisation with freehold can control their environmental aspects, whereas with leasehold they can only influence. This simple model may, however, be complicated in individual cases by the precise nature of the leasing or subletting agreements between parties (*see* Figure 4.2).

Figure 4.2 Some Simple Property Issues in Environmental Management

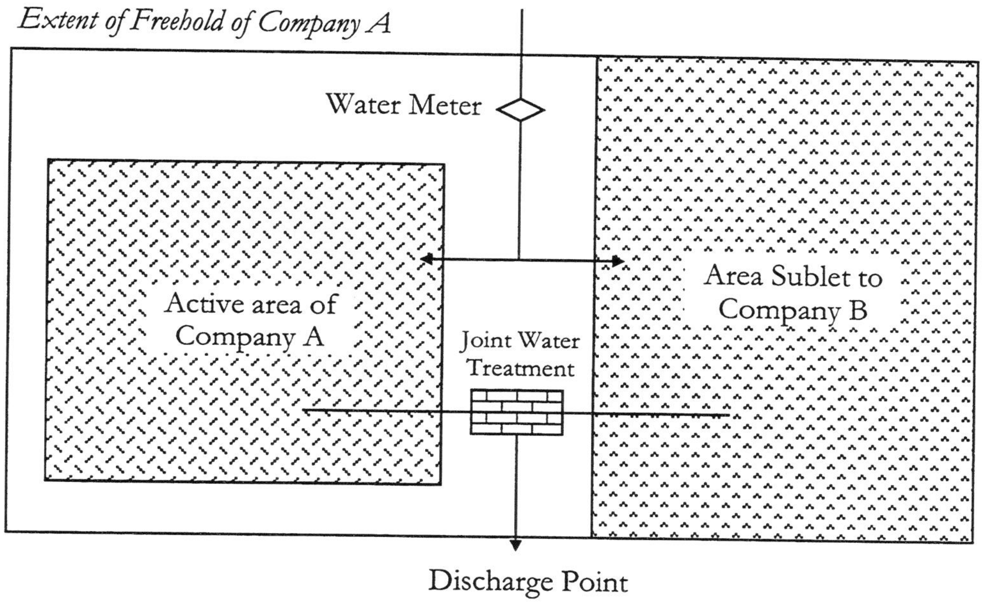

Company A has an effective EMS for its own active area. But effective management of Company B's consumption of water and effect on effluent quality at the discharge point must be undertaken if compliance is to be achieved.

It is surprisingly common to find an organisation occupying land within a complicated structure of ownership and subleasing. This occurrence can lead to difficulties with compliance because individual occupiers are unaware of their precise obligations. Issues which have environmental implications include:

- control of and inputs into communal pollution control infrastructure, such as drainage networks and oil interceptors;

- shared utilities supply;

- risk of causing nuisances;

- shared waste storage facilities;

- bulk storage facilities with uncontrolled access.

Superimposed on these considerations are the legal issues contained in planning consents. All of these make the process of gaining and maintaining sufficient knowledge to manage environmental aspects much more complex.

Environmental Aspects and Impacts Register

According to UKAS the aspects and impacts register is the core of an effective EMS such as ISO14001. It is clear that proper attention to the detail of this stage can save much work later, particularly in the documentation and manuals stage.

Existing Information for Environmental Aspects and impacts

Most companies will have compiled part of, if not all of, an environmental aspects and impacts register as a part of the application/authorisation process under Part I of the Environmental Protection Act 1990 (see section above).

In addition the Environment Agency requires similar undertakings for licensing purposes (both for abstraction and discharge consents). Conditions in the consent will include: limits on composition of the effluent and toxicity, on-site effluent treatment, insitu monitoring, maintenance records and the provision of information. The water undertakers vary in terms of the level of detail required for a consent to discharge to sewer. Nevertheless there is already much information already documented in the company as a result of legal considerations and actions.

Indirect Aspects and Impacts

The legal implications of the aspects and impacts register go further than those laid down in an IPC application/authorisation. In ISO14001 and EMAS there is a requirement to assess the indirect environmental aspects and impacts of the organisation and its product. One example of this indirect environmental effect is in the transportation of products. The system of vehicle labelling for hazardous substances often ignores substances and materials which are not hazardous to human health but are potentially damaging to the environment, particularly the water environment. Examples of 'non-hazardous' products with the potential to pollute the aquatic environment include:

- detergents

- disinfectants

- food stuffs, including dairy products

- beverages

- paint and dyes

- inorganic powders (sand, cement, alum etc.)

- fertilisers

- other organics (e.g. offal, anti-freeze, cooking oil, latex and soluble polymers)

In addition, the company may be required to discuss legal issues relating to non-UK law matters. An obvious example is those companies exporting to Germany and the law relating to responsibility for packaging and packaging waste. In addition it must be remembered that in the European Union there is no restriction on a nation having environmental standards which exceed those laid down in EC directives or regulations (as long as the level does not restrict free trade). So simple knowledge of EC legislation may only be the starting point and may not be relied upon for the specific requirements of a Member State with which an organisation has dealings.

Managing On-Site Contractors within an Environmental Management System

One discrete area of environmental management that needs more detailed review is the management of contractors as an indirect aspect. Running in parallel to environmental concern has been the dramatic changes in business practices by way of 'down-sizing', 'delayering' and 'outsourcing'. As companies have shed staff, in particular middle managers, the pressures and responsibilities on the remaining management have increased with resulting strain on the effective operation of any system. One area in which companies are particularly vulnerable is in the management of on-site contractors.

Increasing Outsourcing

It is a current trend in many organisations to reassess their strategy and look at staffing issues. The result of this is a dramatic increase in the use of outsourced services. Though this is seen as a method devolving responsibility outside the contracting organisation, in practice controls are required to ensure the contractor's staff are aware of their duties. In theory it sounds simple but in practice, particularly in 'delayered' management structures, the additional requirements of environmental legislation are often ignored.

In determining the impact of contractors and in order to prioritise actions to reduce environmental risks, an assessment should be made of the potential legal liabilities presented by their activities. Clearly the differences in exposure to liabilities between a demolition contractor and a cleaning company are considerable. While many of the activities of contractors can be adequately covered as 'abnormal' within an environmental manual, the controls imposed require supervision to a level not currently used, and which may be described within the 'normal' category of operation. There are, as with health and safety, a number of issues to be considered in the management of contractors' environmental effects.

Initial Considerations

Identifying and appointing a suitable contractor should include a consideration of the environmental impact of the activity and the demonstrable expertise in managing and controlling adverse effects. In practice, the appointee will often be known and will have been used in the past. In the case of an organisation which has recently adopted environmental policy aims and objectives, it should reassess suitability in the light of those aims even with known firms. In a constantly changing business and cultural environment experience should not be used as the sole definition of competence.

An initial assessment of priorities for addressing concerns should include the potential of the activity to pollute controlled water and land, to generate waste outside that usually described in waste transfer documentation, to interfere with on-site pollution prevention and control activities and to contravene any consents or permissions. Priority should initially be assigned depending on the significance of the individual environmental effect as described in a register forming a core part of the environmental management system. Attention should also be paid to past problems on the site such as any prosecutions or notices (relating to environmental regulations).

Appointed contractors should be made aware of the corporate environmental policy aims and objectives relevant to the nature of the contract. In practice all environmental policy documentation will be sent as assessing the precise environmental impacts of each contract would create over-complication and potential confusion. It is important to support the documentation with specific references to the contract because the impact of sending out information on preventing environmental pollution of the atmosphere to an office cleaning contractor could be counter-productive.

For large organisations it is good practice to hold seminars for contractors undertaking work identified as having a significant environmental effect to inform them of the policy requirements. Smaller organisations may find this too onerous, but it remains important to assure yourself that these contractors are sufficiently aware of their responsibilities.

The potential impact on a business of poorly managed contractors goes beyond legal liabilities. The profile of a firm can be affected as a result of the poor performance of a contractor. As an agent of the organisation they should be managed as salaried staff. In cases where a contractor comes into direct contact with the general public or customers the exposure increases. In many organisations contractors now carry out a significant number of activities. There is certainly scope to include environmental terms into the contract; however, the damage to the organisation resulting from carelessness or accidental release will have been done. Steps to manage and control more directly these activities are a paramount concern.

Environmental Aspects Evaluation

Contractors in conjunction with a responsible and competent staff member should evaluate the environmental aspects and impacts of an activity. The method of evaluating the significance of the effect should conform to that in general use in a formal EMS. The evaluation should assess the full extent of the potential liabilities. Blaming a contractor for failure to identify all the potential effects is not a constructive response to a pollution event. In light of the sentencing notes in the recent Coalite case (February 1996), which stated clearly that the management in that case could not ignore the responsibility to ensure that instructions were understood and carried out, it is not unreasonable to anticipate that the same is true when managing contractors. It remains the employer's responsibility within the management of environmental effects to ensure a contractor complies with the legal minima and is aware of the company policy.

Abnormal and Emergency Conditions

Many contractors' activities might be managed as abnormal parts of the system and so can be covered in specifically developed documentation. Often contractors are brought in during plant shut-down to undertake annual maintenance. There are many cases of the failure to manage contractors properly in relation to the employer's responsibilities under the Health and Safety at Work Act 1974. The case law can be expected to grow for environmental litigation, and it will not be a surprise if a significant proportion concerns failure to manage contractors.

The performance of contractors under emergency conditions should be of particular concern. Contractors must be aware of contingency plans in the event of an emergency – they may be closest and able to react faster than other staff. Some activities performed by contractors will require emergency plans to be drawn up which are different to the general emergency plans for the site. The recording and analysis of 'near-misses' is vital in determining the extent of the future requirement for emergency plans.

On-site Considerations

Contractors should be briefed prior to the start of each contract. This can be integrated into the health and safety briefing. It is important that the briefing should address the specifics of the contract, and although general environmental awareness should be a long-term aim, it is preferable to concentrate on the immediate requirements of the law. These briefings should be comparable to any on-site staff environmental training which is already in use. Clearly, consistency in terminology and procedures is a basic requirement. On-site staff should be informed through regular briefings when a contractor is working for an extended period as it may well impact on their own function.

Management Control Options

Particular attention should be given to the duty of care imposed by S. 34 of the Environmental Protection Act 1990. This affects all contractors, as it affects all staff, in a number of ways. In practice, especially on large sites, there is a tendency to dispose of waste in a manner inconsistent with the duty of care. This can be a particular problem with contractors. There are a number of management controls which can be used to reduce this problem. As stated above a briefing is the first stage where contractors should be made aware of local rules for waste disposal.

There are, however, additional controls, which can be considered.

- For some activities where the waste generated falls outside the description of waste in the transfer documentation, for example special wastes from demolition or cleansing, or when the expected volume of waste is far greater than normal, then contractors could be required to use their own skip.

- Contractors should be made aware of any labelling of on-site waste receptacles.

- Regular inspections of all waste facilities should be a part of systematic contractor management, to ensure that only permissible wastes are being deposited in the appropriate skip.

- Contractors should be required to indicate in their working plan or scheme of works the nature and amounts of waste materials from the particular job.

Codes of Practice

All tasks may be covered by a code of environmental practice. These can operate in organisations which do not have a formal management system and, indeed, might be considered to be good practice as a starting point in the development of such a system. The code of practice may be a single multi-sectioned document or a set of stand-alone codes. In the later development of system documentation these codes will become the environmental management manual.

Depending upon the nature of the organisation and the target audience, what starts out to be an internal 'voluntary' code of practice may become a public document and therefore in the public's perception mandatory. Any code of practice should be audited, as a matter of good practice itself, so those contractors are aware that it is an important document.

In practice, such codes should be inserted wherever appropriate into existing codes, such as those relating to health and safety or quality. The fewer new documents which are required must be considered to be an advantage in the successful implementation. It must be remembered that the code is designed to reduce legal liabilities associated with the activities of the contractor so effectiveness is the ultimate test.

If codes of practice already exist for health and safety purposes then these should be revisited to include environmental issues. For example, a code for asbestos removal may not contain any guidance on waste disposal.

Off-site Considerations

Although the main focus of this part of the book is the management of contractors working on site, there are occasions when an organisation will appoint a contractor to undertake works off the main site. These might include local authorities appointing contractors to clean out storm water drainage ditches (a scenario which saw a 'spate' of successful prosecutions by the National Rivers Authority in 1995) or the contracted transportation of materials with a potential to pollute.

Contractors should be made aware of the potential and actual environmental impacts of their activities, in exactly the same way as on-site contractors. The major difference between the two types is the nature of management supervision. Clearly there is less scope for *ad hoc* inspections of equipment and practices, but the threat of such visits should exist. This type of approach should apply to a waste contractor, which has specialist considerations and specific legal requirements, but nevertheless management control should extend to include their activities under the duty of care.

Summary

Contracting out has created different management considerations to those normally associated with environmental management. An EMS must address the issue because the potential legal liabilities may become significant. The experiences from health and safety statutory responsibilities and litigation should be used to predict the future for environmental management. Selection of competent contractors, provision of appropriate information in briefings, codes of practice and direct supervision are part of a system for managing and monitoring the environmental performance of key contractors. In most organisations only a small number of contractors will require close supervision.

Organisations which have already achieved ISO14001 or EMAS are presented with increased potential liabilities. In the event of the prosecution of a contractor where insufficient management control was shown to have existed, or worse, to have compounded the problem, it is possible that the standard may be lost.

Environmental Impact Assessment

Although Environmental Assessment (EA) is a separate issue and should not be confused with EMS, there is similarity, particularly in respect of the identification of significant aspects and impacts. EA are required as a part of the formal planning process for major projects, but the principles may be applied to all planning projects. Again one of the benefits of EA at this stage is the identification and appropriate management of significant environmental aspects and impacts. It is clearly the case that legal compliance and long-term cost savings may be obtained through the application of prevention measures at the earliest stages in design and construction.

EA is a statutory requirement in certain cases, but may be built into an environmental policy statement and therefore managed throughout development and commissioning phases in other cases. An organisation might consider including in the guidance on the policy (see above) descriptions of the type of project which would be subject to, as a matter of corporate policy, an EA. This might, for example, be based on capital expenditure on infrastructure or plant, or it may depend on the potential sensitivity of other organisations to the development due to its proximity to housing or schools. This might be particularly relevant in areas where there is a history of nuisance.

Audits and Reviews

There is a mass of information relating to the process of auditing. There is also misuse of the term. An audit is a specific type of activity requiring certain skills. The practice of auditing will verify the effectiveness of the policy and the action programme in achieving the corporate and legal targets. The legal requirements should remain the basis of auditing. However, a huge variety of audits exist.

The key objectives of the environmental audit are:

- to determine the performance of the EMS;

- to determine compliance with all relevant legislation, including health and safety;

- to determine compliance with the corporate objectives and policy;

- to determine effectiveness of internal procedures;

- to determine risks to human health and environment;

- to determine the impact on the environment of the process through appropriate sampling and analysis;

- to advise on improvement programmes.

Ignorance of the legal consequences of pollution is no defence, thus the audit will provide the information from which actions can provide improvements to meet the minimum legal standard. The law provides for breaches as 'one-off' events and for continuous breaches; both may result in heavy fines. For example, in the case of a nuisance (Environmental Protection Act 1990, Part III) fines may be imposed every time a nuisance is shown to have occurred. If this is a daily consequence of, for example, a recent change to the grade of a raw material or fuel, the cumulative costs will be very considerable and may result in plant closure until a remedy is provided. Early identification through the audit process may prevent this from occurring. In the case of 'one-off' pollution incidents, while the penalty will be singular, the regulators will have been alerted to the potential for future breaches (however unlikely). This increased concern may result in the company being required to install and maintain expensive monitoring equipment.

While audit reports are confidential, they may remain *discoverable* documents in the case of prosecution. Consequently, until an organisation is more certain of its ability to respond to the findings of the audit process, it might be advisable to limit the scope of the audit to particular issues. These may be determined by the priorities set by the organisation as a result of the initial review. This is not a matter of secrecy, merely a sensible precaution to prevent too many expensive problems requiring action occurring all at once as a result of the audit. In addition, prior to embarking on the audit process, management should identify a contingency fund to cover expenditure as a result of audit recommendations.

Some audit information and reports may be subject to legal professional privilege. Privilege applies when there is litigation (either actual or predicted) or when legal advice has been sought confidentially from a legal professional in the course of their duties as a lawyer and as an officer of the organisation.

There are many types of basic environmental audit; below is a selection. These can be used for a variety of reasons and with differing repeat cycles.

Compliance Audit

The most common and the one which should have the shortest cycle duration is the compliance audit. The audit checks the extent to which an organisation is complying with existing environmental laws and company policy. This form of audit may, where relevant, be combined with the Environment Agency requirements for regular reporting for IPC authorisation purposes. A more comprehensive compliance audit will examine areas not yet covered by legislation and other standards in an attempt to be more predictive. A practical example is to audit the organisation in terms of European directives not yet enacted in primary UK legislation (*see* Chapter 2). This will provide a form of 'legislation buffer' to allow adjustment to the new requirements. In addition to the general compliance audit, it may be more appropriate to subdivide: waste contractor or 'duty of care' audits are becoming more commonplace (*see* Chapter 2).

The audit should clearly identify areas of legal non-compliance. The auditors should clearly indicate to companies the consequences of not correcting deficiencies which are likely to result in legal breaches. If the audit process is internally resourced, then particular attention should be given to the potential for negligence, on the auditors' part, if this is not done. If external, third-party, auditors are employed then the company must ensure that they are competent and possess sufficient professional indemnity. Finally, it is important to recognise that an audit report may be a legally discoverable document in court proceedings during acquisition.

Process Safety Audit

This type seeks to identify hazards and quantify risks as a direct result of the production process. It might be linked to a health and safety audit with a view to checking accident and emergency procedures, training and readiness. For example, an audit based on the requirements set out in the Operator and Pollution Risk Appraisal (OPRA v.2) from the Environment Agency may provide a useful indication of the performance of a process in terms of safety and environmental criteria.

Occupational Health Audit

This is an examination of the exposure of staff to pollution, noise and temperature. Again there is clear synergy with health and safety audits, thus it should include the provision and use of personal safety clothing, equipment and training in their use.

Product Audit

In effect this is equivalent to a 'life-cycle analysis' (LCA) or in CIA Responsible Care terminology 'Product Stewardship'. This form of audit should assess the 'cradle-to-grave' impacts of the product, including sourcing of raw materials (in particular non-renewable resources), energy consumption at all stages, waste toxicity and management, use and final disposal.

Pre-acquisition Audit

Investigations will focus on significant environmental liabilities (past, present and future) associated with the acquisition. These may include ground contamination and clean-up liabilities, existence of potential litigation (criminal and/or civil) and requirements to achieve BATNEEC. The audit is based on the principle of 'due diligence'.

Reporting (*see also* Chapter 3)

Most authorities accept that reporting is an important part of the EMS. It is an externally assessed part of EMAS. But many companies are worried about commercial confidentiality and as a result remain reluctant to 'go public'. Again, the law has already prepared the way. Under the 1990 directive on freedom of access to information concerning the environment, Member States are required to ensure that certain information held by control authorities and government is available on request to the public. Thus information provided under the Environmental Protection Act 1990 Part I application and authorisation process is held by the appropriate regulator for inspection (IPC and Air Pollution

Control); also discharges to controlled waters, trade effluent and waste management are kept by various agencies. In addition the Environment Agency holds and updates the Chemical Release Inventory which provides information on emissions from IPC sites. Information is available from HMSO through the IPR and PG notes for Part I of the EPA – included in the guidance are sections which identify BATNEEC for each process.

There is enough information already freely available to provide considerable detail about a company (particularly those that are Part I authorised). A company may feel that there is no real constraint on reporting it for yourself. Indeed there may be advantages in terms of PR and, in particular, local community relations.

Summary

EMS is receiving more attention, especially since the launch of ISO14001 in 1996 and EMAS in the spring of 1995. It is a management tool used to reduce the environmental impact of an organisation and provides a structure, responsibilities, procedures and resources for implementing an environmental policy. That policy should be prepared with full cognisance of the legal requirements.

The principles of EMS already exist in the Parts of the Environmental Protection Act 1990 and other legislation. So the progression towards a formal system standard should not be too arduous, particularly in organisations already regulated under Part I of the Environmental Protection Act 1990. The use of EMS as exemplifying expertise is, perhaps, particularly relevant in civil cases. A fully operational, comprehensive EMS will allow an organisation to identify and prioritise improvement programmes in line with environmental legislation requirements. Any organisation establishing or considering establishing an EMS must be aware of the legal consequences – EMS does not represent a 'quick-fix' to statutory environmental compliance.

CHAPTER 5

Taking Effective Action

Information Sources

At the heart of the process of achieving environmental compliance, as stated throughout, is having a clear understanding of the variety of issues which face your company. These include environmental protection legislation (Chapter 2), the new non-statutory pressures (Chapter 3) and compliant environmental management systems (Chapter 4). There is a mass of information and experts who can provide advice. The difficulty is to identify what is important now and in the future from amongst this morass. Everyone seems to be able to offer appropriate guidance, but the company's staff should be undertaking a significant amount of this work. It is, after all, you who know your process best – don't you? The lack of understanding in many of these areas of compliance is becoming increasingly apparent to many working in the area.

Anecdotal evidence shows that when new legislation is formulated industry is thrown into confusion. Such evidence was very apparent during the development prior to implementation of the Packaging Waste Regulations (*see* Chapter 2 for detail). At a seminar I was faced with some senior businessmen who were concerned about the extra work that the anticipated regulations would create. It was the case that most were not monitoring packaging quantities before the enactment of the above regulations. Why was this the case when packaging often constitutes a very significant expenditure for a manufacturing sector company? Such confusion is an unnecessary consequence and should not be a problem for the informed business manager.

I must reinforce the fact that it is the responsibility of the business to make itself aware of all the relevant legislation which will affect it. Many businesses expect the regulatory agencies to inform them of the legislation as it is created or amended. The regulatory agencies take pains to inform as best they can, but it is inevitable that the extension of the scope of environmental legislation to new processes and commercial sectors will make this increasingly expensive.

When we move to consider non-statutory compliance issues, there is no single authority which has the duty to inform the business community. Trade associations are the best placed to perform this role, but their performance in updating on environmental pressures is patchy at best and non-existent at worst. **The organisation best placed to assess the compliance process and its commercial implications is the business itself.**

There are many benefits from environmental compliance, as defined in this book. It is not simply that costs can be reduced to improve profitability. In a world where accountability for one's actions is extending ever farther from the realm of direct control by the business, we must manage a wide range of risks. Reducing those risks provides a greater degree of certainty in a dynamic and turbulent world.

Principles of the Process of Compliance

There is one golden rule that I can offer. Industry must take control of the process of achieving compliance if it is to achieve any significant benefit. Adopting the following simple steps can help to achieve the process of compliance and deliver continuous improvement, to benefit industry itself and the quality of the environment around us.

Understanding the Issues

No organisation can ever attempt statutory and non-statutory compliance without a clear understanding of the range of issues which are of concern. Such knowledge must come from the activities performed in the past, the present and the future. The contents of this book can be distilled into a simple list of the relevant issues, including:

- past land-use to determine the potential for contaminated land;

- present activities which present a potential for causing pollution now and into the future;

- future activities which can be made compliant at the design phase.

There are many sources of information available to assist in the process of compliance. Many guides and manuals exist to help but are rarely used in practice because they are either too simplistic or too complex. The Environmental Technology Best Practice Programme has existed for some five years, has produced hundreds of documents but is still virtually unrecognised in many (if not most) businesses. The Environment Agency produces booklets, posters and videos. And the web has a mass of information on environmental issues and solutions. An industry manager needs to have a clear goal before embarking out on the voyage of discovery; if not they may become overwhelmed with well-meaning, well-written and researched information which they will never use to its fullest or intended extent. Think before taking action – thinking is often an activity low on the list for the increasingly harassed business manager, but one that needs to be performed before any action is undertaken.

Assessing the Risk to the Environment

No organisation can deal at once with all the issues it faces and so must attempt to prioritise the risk to the environment in order to deal with compliance in a logical manner. Figure 1.1 shows that most must start in Box A before moving to gain the extra benefits contained in other boxes. Although the law relating to the environment is immature it is a safe assumption that activities covered by legislation pose a greater risk to the environment than those that are not. It makes sense, therefore, to address statutory environmental compliance issues first – as I have done in this book. Once understood and tackled an organisation may move to comply with the variety of non-statutory compliance issues. As a very simple example it is easier, though not impossible, to report on environmental performance when secure in the knowledge that the company is legally compliant.

Assessing environmental risk must be undertaken in a commercial context; to do otherwise would be unwise. This area will be discussed briefly later in this chapter. There are many processes to determine risk; some have been explored elsewhere in this book. Whichever is chosen, the process must be made relevant to the internal and external issues that must be faced, and it must be repeated at regular intervals. Risk is ever changing: this is ignored at an organisation's peril.

Establishing Programmes to Address Compliance

Environmental management systems provide one way to address compliance. What I hope to have imparted is the view that environmental compliance is not achieved by using a single method, but a combination of approaches, utilising available resources in response to a variety of external factors. Environmental compliance is achieved through a clear vision and with appropriate consultation. Figure 2.4 sets out a model approach to the development of strategies for change in a regulated regime. Programmes have to address external factors by providing an appropriate internal resource and expertise. Many organisations are already looking outwards in the way that they develop and implement programmes, but as accountability grows as a business issue, more must begin to look outwards.

The development and establishment of an effective programme must take account of a huge range of pressures, but should be based on a priority list where options are ranked and targets produced to allow necessary management.

Monitoring and Evaluating Progress

An EMS can provide the structure to allow the monitoring and evaluation of progress. But environmental data management and analysis is one area that I believe remains a weakness in many businesses. In fact I would go further and say that many businesses collect data unnecessarily, in the wrong form, at inappropriate times, with incorrect sampling procedures and using untrained staff. You may get the impression that this is a 'hobby-horse' of mine – and you would be correct. Let me provide you with some simple and real examples.

Most people do not understand that you can describe data using more than one average figure. In fact environmental data is often in a form or of a type that makes complex description necessary. It is not academic distinction but a point of fact. The same data can, for example, be represented using an arithmetic mean and a geometric mean – and give very different answers. If at the heart of your improvement programme you are using inappropriate descriptive statistics to demonstrate success or failure, or compliance, then you can find yourself in difficulty.

The use of units is another area of concern – for example milligram per cubic metre ($mg\ m^{-3}$) is not the same as parts per million (ppm) (and likewise micrograms per cubic metre and parts per billion), although many believe them to be so. Units are especially important when monitoring emissions. A simple misunderstanding can result in serious errors.

Another example of misunderstood data causing problems recently came to my attention. An authorised incinerator used to control solvent emissions was monitored by consultants for NO_x and shown to be over the limit of the authorisation. However, the authorisation limit required NO_x to be measured and expressed as NO_2, not as a combination of NO and NO_2. No one had spotted the problem, not the company, the consultant or the local authority. This may be a detailed example, but it demonstrated the level of competence required by a company if it is not going to set itself undue and unnecessary tasks. It also demonstrates the need to audit the public register to ensure that the company's viewpoint is fairly reflected. This is not a sop to secrecy and an endorsement of lack of disclosure, it is merely good practice.

Many businesses only collect environmental data to demonstrate compliance or show improvement within an EMS. But the cost to the business of gathering and analysing the data, in time and expenditure, may be significant. This process should be able to provide added commercial value, especially in the prediction of changes in response to growth or alteration of processes. The challenge is to integrate the monitoring results and interpretation into mainstream business planning, rather than setting it on one side and treating the environment as an entirely separate issue.

Integration of Environmental Compliance into Business Improvement

External factors are increasingly a part of day-to-day business management. Environmental compliance is only one of many aspects that require effective control and improvement. It requires a degree of technical competence, but for most managing the environment remains a relatively minor element of corporate strategy.

Some commercial activities have an obvious interface with the environment, for example the waste management industry. For these industries the requirement for effective compliance processes is paramount. For others it is less important, but does rear its head from time to time. In both cases the integration of environmental compliance into mainstream business strategy and tactics has become something of a holy grail. At its most basic this involves the simplification of management systems to avoid excessive bureaucracy and provide a consistent process. Depending on the nature of activities, integration can begin with combining environmental compliance with quality management systems or with health and safety risk appraisal and management. It is realistic to expect a business management system to integrate all the non-commercial aspects of running a successful business. This last sentence seems, however, to be something of a contradiction. Running a business is a commercial activity. Running a successful business should include all internal and external aspects, such as quality, health and safety, environment and social factors. By subdividing business management in this artificial way we are avoiding the issue, but providing workable processes to deliver control.

Clear benefits exist for those that can integrate all within business management systems. But progress towards Quality, Environment, Safety and Health (Quensh) is slow. Why should this be the case? I believe that the root cause is internal demarcation and personal politics between technical staff in companies. Call it professional snobbery, if you like, but this will remain a barrier to the development of truly integrated systems until mainstream business management qualifications (e.g. MBAs) take up all these topics. There are a small number of MBA courses that offer electives on environmental or ethical issues, but that is a small number more than two or three years ago.

Moving towards true integration is a complex issue presenting challenges for senior management. With clear goals for environmental compliance these challenges may be simplified to a level that a model can be developed and extended to other areas. This is because unlike most, if not all, other non-financial aspects, the environment presents a huge diversity of problems, challenges and opportunities. Get it right with environmental compliance and progress towards true integration may be acheivable, but fail and the organisation is likely to struggle to achieve this goal.

Establishing Realistic Goals and Expectations

Progress towards sustainable development goals (whatever they are) is going to be slow. It is crucial therefore that action is taken now and not only in response to the latest threat to competitiveness. Businesses that begin to take action now will gain the early benefits of any new activity or venture, notwithstanding that those first in also take the greatest risk. Fear of the unknown is only one of the challenges that needs to be addressed. Another, I believe equally important, challenge is that many in society have unrealistic expectations of what industry can achieve and at what speed. Substantial and sustained change can only be realised through a change in individual and organisational attitudes – which is easier said than done. So the sooner organisations grab the proverbial bull by the horns and make a start, the sooner we all start to see a measurable change in the quality of our environment. I will finish with the following dialogue between trainer and trainee, which I believe shows what it is that we are trying to address.

Trainer: *"Has the principle of polluter pays worked?"*

Trainee: *"No."*

Trainer: *"Why not?"*

Trainee   *"Because all that happens is the cost of pollution control and prevention are passed onto the customer and then eventually to the consumer."*

Trainer: *"I agree. However, who causes the pollution in the first place?"*

Trainee: *"Industry does."*

Trainer: *"Up to a point, but why does industry exist?"*

Trainee: *"To meet the demand for consumable goods from the public consumers."*

Trainer: *"Yes, so would you still argue that the polluter pays principle does not work?"*

APPENDIX

Further Reading

This section of the book does not represent a comprehensive bibliography for the reader, but a selection for those who want to look beyond the brief description and analysis in this book. The books and leaflets contained in this section are those that I have found useful in the preparation of this book, and those that are more generally useful.

Drivers and Barriers

Small Firms and the Environment, Ruth Hillary, published by Groundwork (1995).

Statutory Compliance

Regulatory Realities: The Implementation and Impact of Industrial Environmental Regulation, Andrew Gouldson and Joseph Murphy, published by Earthscan (1998).

The Implications of Water Regulation for Industry, Tony Edwards, published by Stanley Thornes (Publishers) Ltd (1994).

Non-Statutory Compliance

Environmental Management Systems and Cleaner Production, edited by Ruth Hillary, published by John Wiley and Son (1997).

Environmental Liability Insurance, Nick Lockett, published by Cameron May Ltd (1996).

Factor Four: Doubling Wealth, Having Resource Use, E. Von Weizsacker, A.B. Lovins and L.H. Lovins, published by Earthscan Publications (1997).

A Guide to Risk Assessment Management for Environmental Protection, The Department of the Environment, published by HMSO (1995).

Environmental Management Systems

Environmental Management Systems: Principles and Practice, David Hunt and Catherine Johnson, published by McGraw-Hill Book Company (1995).